Miniature Railways
Past and Present

Anthony J. Lambert

DAVID & CHARLES
Newton Abbot   London   North Pomfret (Vt)

British Library Cataloguing in Publication Data

Lambert, Anthony J.
    Miniature railways past and present.
    1. Railroads, Miniature – History
    I. Title
    385'.5   TF675

    ISBN 0–7153–8109–1

Photoset by
Northern Phototypesetting Co, Bolton
and printed in Great Britain
by Biddles Ltd, Guildford, Surrey
for David & Charles (Publishers) Limited
Brunel House, Newton Abbot, Devon

Published in the United States of America
by David & Charles Inc
North Pomfret, Vermont 05053, USA

Front Cover: Excellence in model engineering: the $10\frac{1}{4}$ in gauge Berkshire *The Lady Margaret* on the Stapleford Miniature Railway (*Alan Bowler*)

Title page: A Bassett-Lowke Royal Scot, built in the 1930s, on the $7\frac{1}{4}$ in gauge Spinney Light Railway

CONTENTS

This splendid 10¼in gauge Black Five No 5156 *Ayrshire Yeomanry* will run on what promises to be one of the most beautifully situated miniature railways in the British Isles. The one mile line will run on the Isle of Mull from Craignure (Old Pier) to Torosay where passengers may visit the Victorian baronial castle designed by David Bryce. Construction of the railway began in 1980 and it is expected that the line will be open by the time this book appears. Three steam engines will operate on the line: Trevor Guest's *Ayrshire Yeomanry*, built in 1950, which has worked at Dudley Zoo, Lowestoft, Rhyl and other locations, Curwen freelance Atlantic *Waverley*, built about 1948, which ran as *Black Prince* before moving to Manchester and Loughborough, and a freelance narrow gauge outline 2-6-2T *Lady of the Isles*, built by Roger Marsh and finished in North British Railway livery. During 1981 *Ayrshire Yeomanry* ran on Kerr's Miniature Railway, the first time that steam had regularly worked on the railway since steam ended in 1960. (*Michael R. Oliver*)

INTRODUCTION

Miniature railways are fun; if they weren't, there wouldn't be any. There are many easier, and less worrying, ways of earning a living than running a public commercial railway so nobody would do so unless they enjoyed it; equally the public wouldn't ride on them if they didn't too. The same goes for the many private lines not run commercially. With only one exception (the estate railway at Eaton Hall, built for transporting estate materials) miniature railways have been built to give pleasure to their owners and those who ride on them. Very rarely a miniature railway has served as a functional means of transporting passengers and goods from A to B but this has been an ancillary benefit.

Yet the man who is regarded as the pioneer of miniature railways devoted much of his life trying to convince others that the 15in gauge railway was ideal for military and estate use. Sir Arthur Heywood did not build the first miniature railway – it is uncertain who did – but reliable history begins with his Duffield Bank Railway and there was certainly nobody before him with his sense of mission. He and his family obviously had a whale of a time in the process, entertaining their guests to dinner on the train and even operating a sleeping car train throughout the night! But Sir Arthur built the railway as a demonstration of what could be achieved with 15in gauge. His only convert was the Duke of Westminster's agent, the Hon Cecil Parker, who commissioned Heywood to build a railway to connect the colossal family seat of Eaton Hall with the nearest main line railway station at Balderton. The three-mile line was Heywood's one success, carrying 6,000 tons in its first year.

Retrospectively the most formative influence on the development of miniature railways in this country was probably American amusement park use and its adaptation by Miniature Railways of Great Britain Ltd. This concern was founded in 1904 by W. J. Bassett-Lowke and Henry Greenly, so it was appropriate that the first miniature railway was set up in Northampton where Bassett-Lowke's works were and still are situated. Although the idea of the railway was subjected to criticism from some councillors and a local paper, the public thought otherwise and flocked to ride on this novelty.

The next site was a rather more obvious choice for a recreational enterprise – Blackpool. Again, the venture was a success, but the railway was run on a concessionary basis and at the end of the five year period, in 1910, the lease was not renewed. The Blackpool line established a general rule accepted until after World War II, that the 15in gauge was the minimum suitable for a public miniature railway. Relatively few public lines built before that war were of a smaller gauge, not least because the state of locomotive design in general terms did not enable sufficient power to be developed from a $7\frac{1}{4}$in, or even $10\frac{1}{4}$in, gauge engine. When traffic on Kerr's Miniature Railway at Arbroath exceeded expectations, the decision taken was to increase the gauge from $7\frac{1}{4}$in to $10\frac{1}{4}$in, rather than endeavour to extract substantially more power from a new engine. The question of stability is a quite separate issue. The use of fractional gauges for the smaller sizes arises from the scale ratio to full size with a small amount of gauge widening to give a little more clearance.

The Blackpool line was relaid in the grounds of Halifax Zoo, but meanwhile Bassett-Lowke had discovered another use for the miniature railway – at exhibitions, both at home and overseas. In 1909 Miniature Railways Ltd set up a 15in gauge line at Nancy Exhibition, and others followed, at Roubaix, White City, Brussels, Geneva, Cologne, Breslau and Oslo. Engines of the Little Giant type (the name of the first of a class of 15in gauge 4-4-2s designed by Greenly) were used in all cases, although an enlarged Little Giant, denoted Class 30, was sent to Geneva and Oslo.

Before the company went into voluntary liquidation at the end of 1911 two other lines were opened by Miniature Railways Ltd at Sutton Park in Birmingham and at Rhyl in North Wales. It is evident from subsequent events that the exhibition lines were much more acceptable propositions financially than the fixed lines at holiday resorts or parks; when Bassett-Lowke established a new company, Narrow Gauge Railways Ltd, to promote lines on which to run his products, no effort was made to establish lines in the latter category and the previously-owned lines were sold. Instead Narrow Gauge Railways looked for suitable sites to develop lines that would serve a transport function as well as provide entertainment for tourists.

It was several years before an adaptable opportunity arose. What is extraordinary, in retrospect, is that it was possible for Narrow Gauge Railways to take over two narrow gauge railways in thinly populated areas and convert them to 15in gauge during a world war. Although Bassett-Lowke was on engineering work for the war effort, World War I was clearly not as total an affair as the second. During the latter, some miniature railways were kept going, but generally because they either contributed to the war effort in a positive way, like the Romney, Hythe & Dymchurch Railway, or they provided light relief for war workers in towns or cities at a time when unnecessary journeys were discouraged, of which Sutton Park may be cited as an example.

The first site which Narrow Gauge Railways found was the 3ft gauge Ravenglass & Eskdale Railway in Cumberland. Proctor Mitchell, one of the directors of NGR Ltd, visited the line in 1915 and a three-year lease was signed in the same year. Relaying of the seven mile line began before the agreement was signed, typical of the rather cavalier way in which legal niceties were treated during the early history of the R&ER. (Captain Howey and Henry Greenly were to display equal disdain for legal protocol when setting up the RH&DR.) The railway reopened as far as Muncaster Mill in August 1915 and was open for the full length in the following Spring. It was the longest miniature railway in the country and required locomotives from Duffield Bank to augment what Bassett-Lowke could supply. The Ratty, as the R&ER is popularly known, has proved one of the few miniature railways on which substantial amounts of goods traffic, in the form of stone, has been carried.

In 1916 the Fairbourne Railway in Merioneth received similar treatment, being converted from a 2ft gauge tramway. The association of NGR Ltd with these railways ended in 1924 when Sir Aubrey Brocklebank and a friend acquired the majority of the shares when the company found itself in difficulties. Sir Aubrey immediately sold the Fairbourne, in which he had no interest, but continued to play the role of fairy godmother (or should it be godfather?) to the Ratty until his death in 1929.

Between the wars, there was a notable increase in the construction of railways at seaside and holiday resorts, based upon the rising standard of living for most of the population which made possible the summer holiday or more frequent days at the seaside. Both $10\frac{1}{4}$in and $9\frac{1}{2}$in gauges were used besides 15in, but $7\frac{1}{4}$in gauge was rarely used for public lines until after World War II.

The most important inter-war development was, of course, the construction of the Romney, Hythe & Dymchurch Railway, the most ambitious and the longest miniature railway to be built. Its history is too well known to warrant repetition in a general introduction, but the conception and thoroughness of its execution are a tribute to J. E. P. Howey and Henry Greenly and, it must be said, to the former's financial circumstances. Only once since World War II have comparable means been applied to a miniature railway from the outset – the exceptionally short-lived Réseau Guerlédan, a British inspired 12in gauge line in France; tragically it foundered. It has been possible to adhere to the original concept of the RH&DR, of creating and operating a miniature main line railway, for 50 years. There has been nothing quite like it; perhaps the only comparable line was the short-lived Surrey Border & Camberley Railway on which there was a good section of double track main line with full signalling. It is sadly ironic that Howey's final, rather uninspired choice of location is now threatening the RH&DR's continued existence in the form he would have wished, because of the decline of south-east Kent as a holiday area.

In an area in which diversity and variety are the predominant characteristics, it is difficult to generalise when trying to discern tendencies since the last war. However, it is hardly contentious to assert that the $7\frac{1}{4}$in gauge has become much more important, particularly in the private railway sphere. Naturally the costs of the smaller gauge are likely to be less, and it is well within the capacity of two men to carry a $7\frac{1}{4}$in gauge tank engine, whereas a small $10\frac{1}{4}$in would probably require four and possibly more. A large $10\frac{1}{4}$in gauge tender engine is starting to tax most trailers and may require lifting gear. For the public $7\frac{1}{4}$in railway, the development of locomotive design has effectively negated the objection that large traffic volumes cannot be coped with. The Forest Railroad at Dobwalls in Cornwall carried 170,000 passengers in 1979, with 60–70 passengers per train being well within the capacity of the Union Pacific Big Boy. Equally the one-third scale models of the Lynton & Barnstaple Railway 2-6-2T, built by Milner Engineering, provide another solution to increasing the power output on $7\frac{1}{4}$in.

These two examples represent a fundamental alternative in any gauge: to increase power within the confines of the correct scale for the gauge, or to abandon such considerations and accept only

Above: Sir Arthur Heywood (1849–1916) may be regarded as the pioneer of the 15in gauge and indeed of miniature railways at large. Although engines to that gauge had been built before Heywood began his work, the concept of the miniature railway as a utility was his own. Sir Arthur was the first person to take a first in Applied Science at Cambridge but he was not to pursue a professional career, partly, it is thought, because it was then considered somewhat infra dig for a gentleman to become an engineer. The impetus for Heywood's work was the interest expressed in the idea of a flexible, narrow gauge, trench railway by acquaintances in the Royal Engineers. In 1874 he began to construct at Duffield Bank, his home near Derby, a 15in gauge line (after 9in gauge experiments). Work began on an 0-4-0 tank engine which he completed in the following year. *Effie* is seen here with her creator in 1875. In fact *Effie*, named after Sir Arthur's wife, was not the embodiment of his ideas about 'minimum gauge' engines but a source of power. The only element which was to become a Heywood characteristic was the use of a marine boiler, with cylindrical shell and cylindrical firebox. A tender was constructed to increase its inadequate water capacity. Its fate, unlike its later sisters, is unknown, although it was moved to the family home at Dove Leys near Norbury, Staffordshire, and disposed of in some way in 1911. (*L&GRP*)

Overleaf: One of the most ambitious new railways in recent years has been the $10\frac{1}{4}$in gauge Oakhill Manor Miniature Railway, built to link the car park with the Victorian house which is open to the public. The line was officially opened by Robin Leigh-Pemberton on 16 July 1978. The railway is at present just under a mile long and incorporates unusually heavy engineering works, such as this deep cutting and magnificent bridge. There is a considerable difference in height between the house and car park, necessitating a spiral to gain height. The house itself contains an outstanding collection of ship and locomotive models, including a $9\frac{1}{2}$in gauge 2-6-0 personally built by Col L. B. Billinton who had designed the standard gauge prototype for the London, Brighton & South Coast Railway of which he was chief mechanical engineer. One of the first engines on the Oakhill line was the only $10\frac{1}{4}$in gauge Royal Scot 4-6-0 built by Bassett-Lowke, for Lord Downshire's railway at Easthampstead Park in Berkshire. This superb engine was completed in 1938 and, along with much other equipment from Easthampstead, went to the Hastings Miniature Railway. From Oakhill the engine was expected to go to the USA in 1981. Seen here is the line's Curwen LNER Pacific *Robin Hood.* (see page 87) (*Author*)

stability and the track as criteria for determining the upper limit. The latter course is certainly the cheaper, and a number of narrow gauge designs have appeared with ease of maintenance as a high priority. The choice of American or Continental prototypes in cases where the owner is concerned about scale but seeks a higher output than can be obtained with the smaller British types is obviously significant.

Another notable tendency has been the growth of railways as part of a wider attraction, at a country house or zoo for example, and the creation

Left: Adjacent to Buckfastleigh station on the Dart Valley Railway is the $7\frac{1}{4}$in gauge Riverside Miniature Railway which runs for $\frac{1}{2}$ mile between the standard gauge line and the River Dart. The line opened with $10\frac{1}{4}$in gauge in 1977 and extended to its present circuitous form regauged to $7\frac{1}{4}$in in 1979. Motive power is provided by an ex-Kingsbridge Miniature Railway diesel and *Yeo*, a 4in–1ft (one-third full size) scale model of the Lynton & Barnstaple Railway 2-6-2T of which three were built by Manning Wardle in 1897 (a fourth was added by the Southern in 1925). To an extent, the thinking behind this model and other narrow gauge prototypes of the 1970s has developed Heywood's ideas on minimum gauge by reducing the gauge still further from 15in but has kept the bulk needed for commercial operation by using a large scale. (*Author*)

of railways divorced even from a nearby centre of population which rely almost totally upon the appeal of the railway to draw people off a holiday route or to make a special journey of some distance. Naturally such developments have only been made possible by the increasing car ownership and the mobility it gives.

At the risk of sounding like a disclaimer, the task of writing, however episodically, about the history of miniature railways and locomotives is frustrated by lack of or conflicting documentary evidence. Railways have come and gone without any of their history or details of their engines being committed to paper. With the excellent journals of the Heywood and $7\frac{1}{4}$in Gauge societies, the prospect for future writers about the miniature railway scene is considerably better.

At a time when the proliferation of new standard gauge preservation projects is seen by some as a threat to what has already been achieved, it is perhaps pertinent to consider the situation of miniature railways. There is no reason to suppose that the public miniature railway will escape the changing patterns and prosperity of tourism any more than their full-size counterparts, unless it be that in becoming increasingly price resistant, the customer will favour miniature railways with their generally cheaper fares. Their virtue obviously lies in greatly reduced overheads which should enable most to weather some fall in passenger returns during recessionary times. The impact of the fluctuating fortunes of resorts is another matter, and only time will reveal whether the classic example of a victim of such a downturn in an area's popularity, the RH&DR, will be able to reach a modus vivendi that allows its continued existence in its well-known form.

Nonetheless, the future for public miniature railways seems auspicious; whatever the state of the economy, the general trend towards greater leisure time can only increase the demand for recreational attractions. New railways are opening at a surprising rate, although the spate of construction of highly sophisticated locomotives seems temporarily at an end, Stapleford's Niagara apart. The challenge and pleasures of designing, constructing and operating a complete railway system (in the case of private lines without the commercial constraints of public operation) will doubtless continue to exercise their fascination over creative minds, an appeal that is now over a century old.

Above: The Duffield Bank Railway was completed by 1881 and a most impressive system it must have been. With a ruling gradient of 1 in 10 and a hairpin bend of 25ft radius on the $\frac{1}{4}$ mile branch from the workshops and house up to the main experimental line, the engines must have had to work hard. The main line was $\frac{1}{2}$ mile long in a figure of eight, with three tunnels, a long cutting and a large wooden viaduct. Seen here is Tennis Ground station, the principal station on the line, the passing loop and the three-road carriage shed, with *Effie* on the left. Besides being the personal delight of Sir Arthur, the line was a practical demonstration of the arguments set out in his book *Minimum Gauge Railways*, written to convince others of the merits of the 15in gauge railway for military and estate use. It is sad that after so much effort at publicising his work, Heywood should have had only one victory, the Eaton Hall Railway. Sir Arthur Heywood died suddenly in 1916, and the entire railway was bought at auction by a Derby firm from whom it was immediately requisitioned by the Ministry of Munitions for use in the construction of a new ammunition dump at Gretna Green. *(L&GRP)*

EARLY HISTORY

Below: It was during one of Heywood's 'at home' events in August 1894, when the line was open to visitors for three days, that the Duke of Westminster's agent attended with a view to assessing the suitability of a Heywood railway for the Eaton Hall estate in Cheshire. The power station, central-heating system and conservatories of the Hall consumed 2,000 tons of coal a year and a further 3,000 tons of stores per annum were brought in. A railway connecting the Hall and estate buildings with the Great Western Railway station at Balderton, three miles distant, was an obvious means of transporting such quantities. Sir Arthur did most of the work on the line, surveying it and supervising construction, and the engines and stock were built at Duffield Bank workshops. The line was opened in September 1896 and carried 6,067 tons during the first year. A regular passenger service was never run, although the Hall was open to the public on certain days and received an average of 16,000 visitors a year. However, special trains were run in conjunction with shooting parties and social events at the Hall, and many eminent names appeared in the regular driver's notebook: King Alphonso of Spain, Edward, Prince of Wales, and Winston Churchill. These are the engine sheds in 1896 showing *Katie*. Eaton Railway engines were finished in the Duffield Bank livery of holly green lined out in red and gold. *(L&GRP)*

Above: This is one of the few photographs of either of Heywood's railways which has not been published. It shows *Katie*, formerly *Shelagh*, at Balderton exchange sidings in 1922. When the original *Katie* was sold with *John Anthony* to the Ravenglass & Eskdale Railway in 1916, the plates were removed and fitted to *Shelagh*, the reason being that Constance Edwina Cornwallis-West, known by the family as Shelagh, was no longer the Duke of Westminster's wife. The design for *Shelagh*, an 0-6-0T, was completed in 1898 but it was not until 1904 that the engine was delivered to Eaton Hall. Thereafter the original *Katie* became the second engine, *Shelagh*'s adhesion in all weathers being markedly superior; wet leaves and slippery rails where the line passed through woods were a continual problem. After the first world war, the railway declined; Sir Arthur and William Midgley (Heywood's Engineer for 30 years) had died during the war and the absence of anyone able to maintain and repair the engines led to the acquisition of a Simplex. *Katie* and *Ursula*, the line's other locomotive, were rarely steamed and both were cut up at Balderton in the summer of 1942, the railway being dismantled in 1947. (*L&GRP*)

Top right: The 10¼in gauge Pitmaston Moor Green Railway was operated by two brothers, H. C. and J. A. Holder, in the grounds of the family home at Moor Green, Birmingham. Built in about 1898, the railway was in the form of an oval with a triangular junction on one 'side' leading to a branch that crossed over the line on the opposite side of the oval. The line included a 27yd tunnel. Three engines operated on the line: a Great Northern 4-2-2 with Belpaire firebox, a 'Yankee' 4-4-0 built by the Holders' mechanic, Grimshaw, and a 4-2-2 single described as Great Western although its outline seems to have owed as much to Pollitt's Class 13 design for the Great Central, which appeared in 1900, as may be judged from this photograph of it. The boilers on the three engines worked to 100lb/sq in and steam was raised by a gas jet lighting a bed of charcoal; anthracite was added as soon

as the blower could be turned on. The engines were fitted with Schaffer & Budenberg injectors; the GW single had two pumps worked off the crossheads while the other two had axle pumps. (*Birmingham Reference Library*)

Right: Captain J. A. Holder's later 10¼in gauge railway ran for ½ mile round his home, Keeping, at Beaulieu in Hampshire. The Atlantic *John Terence*, named after Captain Holder's son (who in later years was involved with the miniature railway at Wembley Exhibition in 1924/5 and with the Romney, Hythe & Dymchurch Railway), was built about 1908 in Captain Holder's workshops at Broome, near Stourbridge, by his engineer, Mr Grimshaw. Although based on the Great Northern Atlantics, the engine was not to scale, having a larger wheelbase, bigger driving wheels and a higher pitched boiler than an exact scale equivalent. The engine had a pull-out regulator and was fitted with an adjustable steam nozzle injector designed by Henry Lea, a Birmingham consulting engineer who had a railway round his garden at Edgbaston in Birmingham. (Henry Lea was one of the select few present at the trials of *Little Giant* on the Eaton Railway in 1905.) *John Terence* was rebuilt with Walschaert's valve gear, outside steam pipes and top feed and is seen here in this form in 1934. After the railway at Keeping was disbanded, *John Terence* went to the Stonecot Hill Railway at Carshalton in Surrey on which it ran as a 4-4-4 with a new cab. Other locomotives on the Keeping Railway were a Baltic tank named *Mary*, built by Bullock in 1932 and a Pacific *Audrey*, again built by Bullock, using parts from a 4-6-4 designed by Captain Holder in 1912. During the second world war *Audrey* was lent to the War Office to show commandos how best to place explosives on locomotives. After the war, *Audrey* went to Dudley Alexander's line at Brockenhurst where she ran as a 4-6-4. The bridge in the background was fabricated at the Earl of Dudley's ironworks for Captain Holder's first railway at Broome. (*Courtesy the Earl of Leicester*)

Above: This old, faded, but historic photograph shows the first 15in gauge public railway in Great Britain, the Blackpool Miniature Railway, opened by Miniature Railways Ltd along the South Shore on 10 June 1905. The irregular circle of 433yd was operated by *Little Giant*, the first of Bassett-Lowke's notable 15in gauge 4-4-2s which had been ready for shop trials at Northampton on 25 April 1905. It must have been an exciting week for the Bassett-Lowke staff as the previous Saturday, 20 April, had seen the opening of the 10¼in gauge line in Abingdon Park, Northampton, worked by George Flooks' 0-4-4T *Nipper* which later went to the Sutton Miniature Railway. The Blackpool line was a commercial success although the line's proximity to the sandy beach resulted in badly worn bearings and motion. Another difficulty was caused by the vogue for women to wear hats resembling a cornucopia: sparks from the engine caused damage and, on one occasion, a conflagration! After five years the concession from Blackpool Corporation expired and in 1910 the line was moved to Halifax Zoo which had been set up in the previous year at Chevin Edge. (*H. Armitage*)

Below: The original *Little Giant* of 1905 is obviously one of the most historic miniature engines. Designed by Henry Greenly following no particular British outline and built by Basset-Lowke for the first 15in gauge public line in Great Britain, at Blackpool, No 10 *Little Giant* was transferred to Halifax Zoo with the rest of the Blackpool railway in 1910. When this line, too, closed in 1914, *Little Giant* was put in store at Northampton until 1922 when she was rebuilt with a new boiler from Allchin & Sons and put up for sale. Her purchaser was a Mr Bunce who built a line in his amusement park at Sunny Vale, Hipperholme, near Halifax. The line closed in 1948 and *Baby Bunce*, as No 10 was named at Hipperholme, was bought by R. Dunn of Bishop Auckland. After an overhaul and another change of name, to *Robin Hood*, No 10 went to the South Shields Miniature Railway where it ran until closure of the amusement park.

Had it not been for the enthusiast grapevine, the original *Little Giant* would have been scrapped by South Shields Corporation which was redeveloping the park. Thankfully it was found and rescued by Mathew Kerr.

Little Giant was restored over two years by its present owner, Tom Tate. In 1965 *Little Giant* went to the Ravenglass & Eskdale Railway for trials but sadly her narrow wheel treads prevented running beyond Ravenglass station limits. However, at a ceremony on 12 September 1965, No 10 was renamed *Little Giant* by Ernest Steel, the son-in-law of Henry Greenly. *Little Giant* is seen here at Ravenglass. (*D. Rodgers*)

Right: The 15in gauge Lakeside Miniature Railway at Southport was originally promoted by an enterprising postman, G. V. Llewelyn. He commissioned Miniature Railways Ltd and Henry Greenly to build and equip the ½ mile line which ran along the south side of Marine Lake. Bassett-Lowke Little Giant No 18 *George the Fifth* was the first engine but was sold to the railway at Rhyl when a Class 20 Improved Little Giant No 21 arrived in 1912 from Northampton, named *Prince Edward of Wales*. The improved engines were the outcome of the tests with *Little Giant* at Eaton Hall in 1905, which suggested to Greenly that more power was needed to work an amusement park line. Accordingly the boiler and cylinders were enlarged and a grid superheater added. The external appearance was changed by having straight splashers and outside bearings for the pony truck to protect them from ashes. The basic Little Giant feature of short coupled-wheelbase to negotiate fairly sharp curves was retained. The buildings on the Southport line were in the rustic style of the station in this photograph of *George the Fifth*. The rolling stock was built by Bassett-Lowke. There were two types of open bogie coaches with reversible seats, and four, roofed, 12-seat bogie coaches with glass screens at each end. The absence of run round loops meant that the train had to be propelled in one direction which may have been the reason behind the provision of lights on the carriage ends. Only the small tail light may be seen above the driver in this photograph but a larger headlight was provided beneath it. (*J. K. Williams collection*)

BASSETT-LOWKE SETS THE PATTERN

Right: Taken between 1919 and 1922, this photograph of Little Giant Class 20 No 2 (Southport numbering — Bassett-Lowke No 21) *Prince Edward of Wales* is of particular interest since Sir Arthur Heywood's *Katie* is just visible behind the weatherboard of the coach. *Katie* was designed for light loads over short distances so it was not surprising that successive owners found her to be unsatisfactory when they applied her to unsuitable work. *Katie* was bought, together with *John Anthony*, from the Eaton Railway in 1916 by the Ravenglass & Eskdale Railway where the steep gradients proved too much for her marine-type boiler, giving her a reputation for poor steaming. In 1919 *Katie* was sold to Llewelyn's but she was to remain at Southport for only three years before being exchanged for Class 20 Improved Little Giant No 22 *Prince of Wales* which the Fairbourne Railway had owned from new. In common with the other engines on Llewelyn's Miniature Railway, names and numbers were changed without any thought to the trials future historians would have endeavouring to sort out fact from fiction! Moreover Bassett-Lowke was not averse to renaming and renumbering after overhaul and duplicating names. At least four Little Giant engines carried the names *Prince of Wales* or *Prince Edward of Wales* at various time. (*J. K. Williams collection*)

Above: One of the earliest public miniature railways was the line in Sutton Park, Birmingham. Opened in 1906, the fun-fair was given the name 'Crystal Palace' because of a large winter garden-type of building which formed the main attraction. In the previous year, W. J. Bassett-Lowke had opened a 10¼in gauge line in Abington Park, Northampton; it was this line which was relaid in Sutton Park and opened with the Abington Park locomotive and stock for the summer of 1907. The engine was 0-4-4T *Nipper*, built by George Flooks of Watford to a design by Henry Greenly based upon the Metropolitan Railway Class E engines. *Nipper* had operated on a line at Bricket Wood near St Albans which Flooks opened with Fred Smithies, who invented a type of locomotive boiler and later became a driver at Blackpool and Rhyl. The Bricket Wood line closed in the summer of 1904 after Flooks broke a leg, and *Nipper* was sold to Bassett-Lowke by Smithies. *Nipper* was made redundant when the line at Crystal Palace was regauged to 15in during the winter of 1907–8. (*J. Tidmarsh collection*)

Below: After regauging the Crystal Palace line to 15in, Bassett-Lowke provided the second Little Giant No 11 *Mighty Atom*, finished in Midland Railway red, to work the line. Of approximately 1000ft in length, the line ran in an almost straight line with run-round loops employing spring points at each end. To save the driver effort, a device enabled him to operate the locomotive and tender couplings from the cab. A change of motive power on the Crystal Palace line was occasioned by events across the Channel. In 1909 Bassett-Lowke set up a line at the Exposition Internationale de l'Est de la France at Nancy, sending the third Little Giant No 12 *Entente Cordiale*. Traffic proved so heavy that a second engine was required, compelling Bassett-Lowke to send *Mighty Atom*, repainted in GNR livery and renamed *Ville de Nancy*. To run trains at Sutton Park, one of the two Cagney 4-4-0s on the Blakesley Hall Railway near Towcester, Northamptonshire, was borrowed for the rest of the 1909 season. The Cagney 4-4-0s were based on a New York Central Railway prototype, No 999, which was claimed to have reached 112mph on the Empire State Express in 1893, creating a new world speed record. Little credence is now given to this. The Blakesley Hall Cagney is seen here on the Crystal Palace line. (*Sutton Coldfield Library*)

Above: Mighty Atom returned to the Crystal Palace railway but the history of the line during and immediately after the first world war is shrouded in mystery. However, in 1920 *Mighty Atom* was bought by Llewelyn's Miniature Railway at Southport and thoroughly overhauled in the following year, receiving continuous splashers and a new name, *Prince of Wales*. In 1929, it was purchased by Nigel Parkinson who, with his father, built an extensive 15in gauge railway at Yarmouth. *Prince of Wales* was rebuilt with smoke deflectors and, like the Improved Little Giants, outside bearings on the pony truck to obviate the wear caused by firebox ashes falling onto the original inside bearings. The Parkinsons also operated a railway at Southend-on-Sea (on which *Synolda* from the Sand Hutton Railway ran) and *Prince of Wales* was used on the Essex line. In 1937 the Yarmouth Miniature Railway closed, whereupon the track and most of the rolling stock was purchased by Pat Collins, the lessee of the Crystal Palace, to reopen the railway at Sutton Park. So *Prince of Wales* returned to its first home; it is seen here at Crystal Palace station on 7 August 1939, still in YMR livery. The driver is C. D. Priestley who drove at Sutton on an irregular basis from 1938 to 1948. *Prince of Wales* was finally retired in 1953 and is currently in store. (*L. W. Perkins*)

Below: Before the first world war, Douglas Clayton, who was a director of Cannon Ironfoundries at Bilston, purchased plans and castings for a Class 30 Atlantic from Henry Greenly/Bassett-Lowke. Construction began in Clayton's own workshop but was terminated by the outbreak of war. It was 1930 before work was resumed, but by this time the drawings had been lost, so it was as a freelance design that *Douglas Clayton* emerged from the works in 1933, finished in Brunswick green with Great Western on the tender sides. This engine ran on Clayton's line at Hardwicke Manor near Tewkesbury. A second engine of the same design was begun in 1938 but again war intervened. Before the engine could be completed, Mr Clayton died, in 1946, and the whole railway was sold to T. G. Hunt. *Douglas Clayton* was overhauled at Hunt Brothers' works at Oldbury after a season's work on the newly named Sutton Miniature Railway. She was renamed *Sutton Belle* and finished in red with yellow and black lining. The partly built engine was completed for Easter 1952, being named *Sutton Flyer* and finished in Royal blue livery with yellow and black lining. In 1959 she visited the RH&DR, although the lack of vacuum brake equipment prevented use on service trains. *Douglas Clayton* is seen here on the Hardwicke Manor line. (*L&GRP*)

Above: Pat Collins requested Harold Parkinson to lay out the new line at Sutton. The new railway incorporated the original line but the route was lengthened to provide a journey of about 1,000yd. At the Crystal Palace terminus, the covered station, parts of which came from Yarmouth, doubled as an engine and carriage shed. The line functioned after a fashion during the war but, with minimal maintenance, it was in a sorry state by 1946. In 1948 the railway was acquired by T. G. Hunt who inaugurated a series of improvements that were to create one of the most efficient miniature railways in the country. This photograph was taken on Easter Monday 1958, showing *Sutton Belle*, with John Ward driving, running into the station with the three coach Yarmouth Miniature Railway set; on the left is *Sutton Flyer* with Bill Hunt on the footplate, waiting to couple on to the train and leave tender first. *Sutton Belle* will then run back through the station to stand clear of the crossover to wait for the next train. With three engines and two train sets, passenger flows of 1,500 an hour were handled. Usual Bank Holiday figures were 6–8,000 but the record was achieved on Whit Monday 1960 when just over 12,000 people were carried in 11 hours. Tragically the line closed on 7 October 1962 with the termination of the lease for the whole of the Crystal Palace site, which the local council would not renew. (*J. Tidmarsh)*

Right: The 15in gauge miniature railway round Marine Park at Rhyl in North Wales was one of the earliest of the seaside lines. It was opened on 1 May 1911 in time for the Bank Holiday weekend after only five months of construction work. Financed by Miniature Railways Ltd on a concessionary basis, the railway was surveyed and designed by Henry Greenly and his apprentice draughtsman Henry Adrian Brough. Beginning the survey work in December 1910, Greenly described it as an ideal site. It proved equally good from the commercial viewpoint, 5,003 passengers being carried on August Bank Holiday Monday in 1911. On the opening day so many people wanted to ride on the footplate that a special fare of one shilling for adults and sixpence for children was introduced. Among those who availed themselves of this opportunity was the Earl of Grosvenor whose father, the Duke of Westminster, had commissioned one of the first 15in gauge railways (see page 11). Both Albert Barnes, the manager, and Fred Smithies, the driver, must have added great character to the railway: Barnes was renowned for wearing a stetson long before they were made familiar by the cinema, and Fred Smithies, whose wife ran his dairy business in Watford while he drove trains, was often accompanied by his dog who enjoyed riding round on the tender. In 1912 Miniature Railways Ltd went into liquidation and the operators of Marine Lake Amusement Park, Rhyl Amusements Ltd, took over the one mile line. They made a number of improvements, including the construction of a new tunnel, engine shed and new bogie coaches. By 1913 it was evident that the two Bassett-Lowke Little Giants with which the line was worked, No 15 *Prince Edward of Wales* and No 18 *George the Fifth* (from Southport), were inadequate for the traffic. Accordingly, Albert Barnes asked Henry Greenly to design a new Atlantic which A. Barnes & Co of Rhyl, the family business, would manufacture at their Albion Works. The war prevented construction starting until 1920. The first of the six engines, No 101 *Joan*, is seen here on a well-laden train. The railway closed after Rhyl Amusements' lease expired at the end of 1969. The line has been reopened and one of Barnes' engines was at work in 1979. At the time of writing, a Rhyl businessman has managed to assemble four of the other Barnes' engines and intends that all six should return to Rhyl. This would be the first time all six were united since No 104 *Billie* went to Margate Dreamland Railway when new in 1928. (*Graham Ellis collection*)

Miniature Train, Ma[...]

Right: Fully covered and walled stations on miniature railways are rare. A notable exception is the station at Rhyl which owes little to Henry Greenly's original design. The station is seen here on 27 August 1954 in the form it took following reconstruction between the wars. Worthy of note are the smoke ducts which must have required the use of the blower to have been of any benefit! An unusual characteristic of the railway's rolling stock was that all the seats faced the same way, made feasible of course by the circular layout. One of the publicity postcards produced just after the first world war revealed that the railway's inspector, Charles Waterfield, had enlisted after 50 years on the stage, giving his age as 43! (*H. C. Casserley*)

Lake, Rhyl

Above: The Ravenglass & Eskdale Railway opened in 1875 as a 3ft gauge line to facilitate the extraction of iron ore deposits in Eskdale which had been worked on and off since Roman times. For 38 years it performed its function in a perfunctory and impecunious manner until the mine workings which it served were flooded in December 1912; the 3ft line ran for another four months in the vain hope that the mine would be reopened, finally closing on 30 April 1913. With the experience of the second world war in mind, it seems extraordinary that the earlier world war should have allowed the time for the creation of a tourist railway, for in 1915, Narrow Gauge Railways Ltd, under the aegis of W. J. Bassett-Lowke and Robert Proctor Mitchell, began to reopen the line in sections after regauging to 15in. The first engine was Class 30 Little Giant No 31 *Sans Pareil* which had operated on a line at Christiania (Oslo) as *Prince Olaf* and quite possibly at Geneva before that. This photograph of *Sans Pareil* shows two Heywood coaches. (*W. A. Camwell collection*)

15in GAUGE – A MEANS OF TRANSPORT

Top right: On 31 May 1916 the equipment of the Duffield Bank Railway was auctioned and purchased by a Derby firm. The locomotives and track were requisitioned by the Ministry of Munitions with a view to using them to construct an ammunition depot near Gretna Green. Whether they went north is not absolutely certain but in the summer of 1917 *Ella* and *Muriel* were delivered to Ravenglass in covered motor lorries. The yard crane could manage *Ella* but *Muriel* required the Furness Railway breakdown crane to unload her. *Ella* had entered service in 1881 and was the first engine to embody all Sir Arthur's theories about 'minimum gauge' locomotives. Heywood's radial valve gear, to overcome the problems arising from a rigid wheelbase, was to prove a drawback on the R&ER, causing oscillation. Although powerful enough for the stone trains and excursion traffic, *Ella* consumed four times as much coal as the miniature scale engines did coke. This may have been the reason for the proposal that she should be converted to oil-firing. In the event *Ella* was converted from an 0-6-0T to a 2-6-2 powered by a Lanchester car engine, her final run as a steam engine being on 5 September 1926. *Ella* is seen here with Bert Thompson, her regular driver, at Ravenglass in 1924. (*Ravenglass & Eskdale Railway*)

Below: When *Ella* was withdrawn, she was 45 years old and in need of a major rebuild. ICL No 2, or 'the Lanchester' as it was commonly known, was created by mounting a Lanchester Model 38 touring car chassis on *Ella*'s frames and wheels. To allow equal speeds in both directions, a Parson's Marine direct reverse gear was fitted and connected to the worm drive by a universal joint. The rebuild proved a success, pulling heavy loads and capable of a reasonable speed. A head-on collision with ICL No 1 in October 1928 damaged No 2's frame with lasting effect, and a big end went through the crankcase in the following year. Spare parts proved virtually unobtainable and she was withdrawn. Her demolition was a very gradual process, the frames still languishing at Murthwaite in 1960. (*W. A. Camwell collection*)

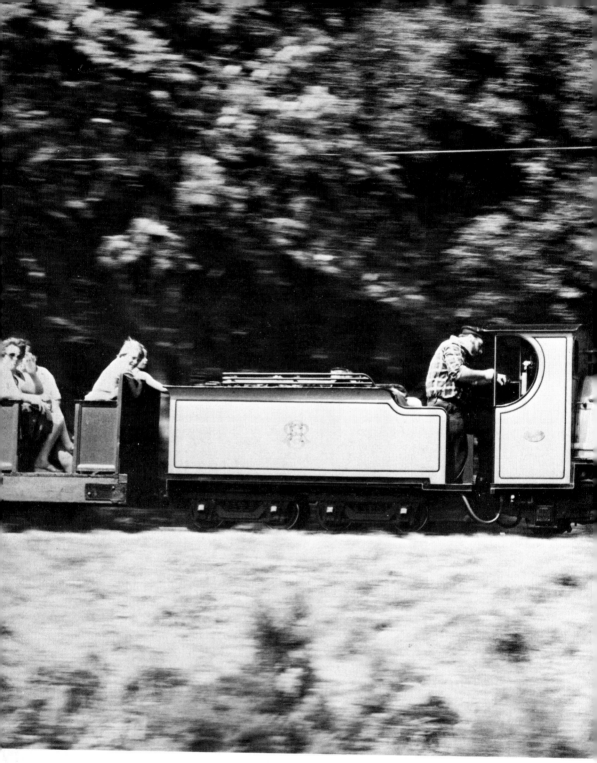

The most recent new engine on the R&ER is *Northern Rock*, a 2-6-2 designed largely by the Chief Engineer of the railway, Tom Jones, and his successor, Ian Smith, with ideas from various sources. Originally an 0-8-2 was projected but trials of RH&DR *Northern Chief* in 1971 prompted a reconsideration of the wheel arrangement and other features. RH&DR influence may be seen in the regulator and Cartazzi radial axle. The boiler was made by Hunslet, the frames by Frazer of Hebburn and the cylinder castings by Heathcotes of Cleator Moor. The rest of the work was carried out at Ravenglass. *Northern Rock* was commissioned on 29 May 1976, the railway's centenary year, and is seen here at milepost 6 on 16 August 1976. She is finished in a slightly greener shade of the 'improved engine green' which Stroudley devised for the Highland Railway. (*P. H. Groom*)

Above: Despite the construction of six 15in gauge bogie bottom-discharge wagons by the Yorkshire Engine Co, the transhipment arrangements for the stone traffic at Ravenglass which resulted from the development of new quarry faces after the first world war inevitably proved a source of delay and inconvenience. Accordingly a $2\frac{1}{2}$ mile standard gauge branch was built to Murthwaite in 1929, construction being carried out by the company in the remarkably short time of eight months, albeit utilising the trackbed of the 15in gauge line in most places. The 15in was relaid between the rails of the standard gauge, as may be seen in this photograph of *River Irt* approaching Mill Wood with a train for Ravenglass. The granite traffic from Murthwaite ended in 1953. *River Irt* was a major reconstruction of Heywood's 0-6-0T *Muriel* which by 1927 was in need of a new boiler. It was decided to make her an 0-8-2 by lengthening the frames and to fit a miniature scale boiler which was made by the Yorkshire Engine Co. Sir Arthur would have been gratified that the new cab afforded the minimal protection for the driver that he considered appropriate. This defect was remedied in 1972–3 when a taller cab, dome and chimney were fitted. Her Heywood valve gear was retained. (*C. M. Whitehouse collection*)

Above: *Sir Aubrey Brocklebank*, named after the chairman of the Cunard Line and saviour of the R&ER who lived at nearby Irton Hall, was the one and only engine built by Hunt & Co of Bournemouth, in 1919. The engine was an enlargement of *Colossus* which had been designed by Greenly in 1914. The 'consulting engineer' of the railway, W. V. Cauchi, claimed to have had a hand in the design but it is unlikely that he did more than specify a larger boiler. The third and last of the 'correct' $\frac{1}{4}$ scale engines on the R&ER, *Sir Aubrey Brocklebank* suffered from the same defects as the other two – insufficient strength, her frame physically breaking in 1926. She was finished in light blue, Midland red and green successively. At the end of 1927 she was withdrawn and amalgamated with *Colossus* to form *River Mite*. (*W. A. Camwell collection*)

Below: *River Esk* in her original form outside the shed at Ravenglass. Designed by Greenly in collaboration with Proctor Mitchell, *River Esk* was built in 1923 by Davey Paxman and had the distinction of two 'firsts' in British locomotive history: it was the first 2-8-2 design and the first engine to be fitted with Lentz poppet valve gear. Invented by Dr Hugo Lentz in Czechoslovakia, the first British standard gauge application of the valve gear was by Gresley on two NER Atlantics and from the design stage on the D49 Hunt class 4-4-0s. Built to $\frac{1}{3}$ scale, *River Esk*'s proportions enabled it to cope with the heavy stone trains for which it was designed. However, the Lentz valve gear did not prove a success and it was completely rebuilt in 1927 by the Yorkshire Engine Co which constructed a steam tender on the Poultney articulated system, using Walschaerts valve gear. The Poultney system was not a success either and the tender was rebuilt in conventional form in 1931, its height marring the original attractive appearance. The tender has since been rebuilt. Originally finished in green livery, *River Esk* is now in blackberry black. (*W. A. Camwell collection*)

Left: In 1927, the Bassett-Lowke Class 60 Little Giant 4-6-2 *Colossus* (formerly *John Anthony* of the Staughton Manor Railway) and *Sir Aubrey Brocklebank* were withdrawn, stripped to the frames and running gear and placed back to back to produce an articulated locomotive. The pony trucks were removed to allow room for the Belpaire firebox of the larger boiler built by the Yorkshire Engine Co to supply the four cylinders. Thick side plates connected the boiler and tender and both units were pivoted. Flexible pipes fed steam to the cylinders and the exhaust from the rear pair was routed through a feedwater heater on the tender tank. The power of *River Mite* was perfectly adequate for stone and passenger trains but proved too much for the frame structure, distortion becoming so serious that the engine was withdrawn at the end of the 1937 season and partly dismantled before intended rebuilding. The second world war prevented this and the chassis were sold to A. Barlow of Southport. *River Mite* is seen here at Ravenglass. (*W. A. Camwell collection*)

Bottom left: The second *River Mite* was the Ravenglass & Eskdale Railway's first new engine for 44 years. Since the reopening of the line after the second world war, in the summer of 1946, the railway had relied upon *River Esk* and *River Irt* and three diesels. In 1963 the R&ER Preservation Society decided to raise money for a new locomotive, and the order was placed with H. Clarkson & Son of York later that year. The wheels, frames and motion of the Poultney tender from the 1928 rebuild of *River Esk* were utilised. The design was developed from the original drawings of *River Esk* but adopted equalised springing on the driving wheels, a heavier pony truck and a Cartazzi trailing axle. Construction had begun by the end of 1964 and the engine was completed in November 1966.

Haulage from York to Ravenglass was by a Burrell showman's engine *Providence*. *River Mite* was named at a ceremony at Ravenglass on 20 May 1967 and is seen here on the turntable at Hythe during a visit to the RH&DR in October 1980. She is finished in Furness Railway Indian red. (*P. H. Groom*)

Below: The recent history of the R&ER, involving its rescue by the Ravenglass & Eskdale Railway Preservation Society and Colin Gilbert in 1960, is well known, and the railway has gone from strength to strength. An annual visit to the railway will almost invariably reveal a major improvement, whether it be structural or in terms of the rolling stock or operating procedures. To commemorate the railway's centenary in 1976, a cavalcade of locomotives was organised for Saturday 25 September. Visiting engines included the original *Little Giant*, former Blakesley Miniature Railway petrol driven, steam outline 4-4-4T *Blacolvesley*, and *Dr Syn* from the RHDR. Four other visitors are seen here on an empty coaching stock working leaving Miteside loop where there was once a halt with upturned sailing boat for shelter: from left to right, W. P. Stewart's No 4472 *Flying Scotsman*, built in 1976, *Count Louis* and *Siân* from the Fairbourne, and Krupp Pacific No 1662 *Rosenkavalier* from Bressingham. (*D. Rodgers*)

FAIRBOURNE MINIATURE TRAIN & BARMOUTH.   200647 (V)

Above: When Arthur McDougall of self-raising flour fame began to develop what is now Fairbourne on the southern bank of the Mawddach Estuary opposite Barmouth, a 2ft gauge tramway was built to carry construction materials. After this traffic ceased, passengers were carried to Penrhyn Point from where ferries ran to Barmouth. In 1916 Narrow Gauge Railways Ltd bought the line and converted it to 15in gauge, using the original track. A station, engine shed and signalbox were built at Beach Road, and services commenced with Bassett-Lowke Little Giant No 22 *Prince of Wales*. The inter-war years saw two changes of ownership and the acquisition of several historic engines, including Heywood's *Katie* from Llewelyn's Miniature Railway and the 18in gauge Stirling Single built at the Regent Street Polytechnic (see page 63). By the time *Katie* reached the FR, she was almost life-expired and proved so unreliable that she was withdrawn and largely scrapped in 1926, all that remains being her frames which may be seen in the Museum at Wharf station, Tywyn. After the second world war, the line was rescued from its run down state by three West Midlands industrialists and gradually brought up to the present standard. This early photograph shows *Count Louis*, a Bassett-Lowke Class 30 Little Giant, near Penrhyn Point.

Top right: Count Louis Zborowski was the son of a wealthy American who became a naturalised British subject and in his twenties, a successful racing driver. At Brooklands he won numerous races in his 2.3 litre Mercedes-Maybach that was known as Chitty-Chitty-Bang-Bang. Another of his interests was miniature railways, and it was for the 15in gauge line being built at his home at Higham near Canterbury that Zborowski bought Bassett-Lowke Class 30 No 32 in 1924. The engine was assembled in the previous year with frames and castings made in 1914, while Allchin & Sons, the traction engine manufacturers of Northampton, built the boiler. It was the last 15in gauge engine to be built by Bassett-Lowke. The engine was purchased as a stop-gap since Zborowski had ordered two Pacifics to a design by Henry Greenly which had been commissioned jointly by Zborowski and Captain J. E. P. Howey. On 19 October 1924 Zborowski was tragically killed when his Mercedes hit a tree during the Italian Grand Prix at Monza. Howey took delivery of the two Pacifics (later RH&DR Nos 1 and 2) from Davey Paxman & Co of Colchester, but the Atlantic was bought by the Fairbourne Railway where it was fittingly named *Count Louis*. The original superheater has been removed and the engine has been substantially rebuilt. *Count Louis* is seen here at Fairbourne on 12 October 1980 with Leslie Vaughton who has driven it since new. (*Author*)

Right: Fairbourne 2-4-2s *Siân* and *Katie* passing on the FR's intermediate loop on 12 October 1980. Built in 1950 by Trevor Guest for the Dudley Zoo Railway, *Katie* was designed by Ernest Twining and was to be the basis for *Siân*. Although intended for the Dudley Zoo Railway, *Katie* was purchased by Captain Vivian Hewitt of Anglesey with a view to sending it to the West Indies to operate on a line which he was planning to create on his sugar plantation. Before this was put into effect, Captain Hewitt died, leaving a collection of over 30 7¼, 9½ and 10¼in gauge engines, and the Fairbourne Railway purchased its second *Katie* in 1965. (*Author*)

Top left: After World War II, the $10\frac{1}{4}$ in gauge Dudley Zoo Railway was regauged to 15in. Trevor Guest, who had built locomotives for Dudley Zoo before the war, provided two new engines, *Ernest W. Twining* and *Prince Charles*. The former was a freelance Pacific to Twining's design, with 20in driving wheels, two $5\frac{1}{16}$ x 8in cylinders and piston valves. When the line at Dudley Zoo abandoned steam in 1957, both engines became redundant and were placed on loan with the Fairbourne Railway, *Prince Charles* in 1960 and *Ernest W. Twining* in 1961. *Prince Charles* left the FR in 1962 but the Pacific has remained to add a welcome touch of Caledonian blue to the green of the other Fairbourne engines. It is seen here at Fairbourne on 26 July 1972. (*P. H. Groom*)

Left: Siân was the first engine to be designed specifically for the terrain through which the Fairbourne Railway runs. Sand is anathema to unprotected precision engineering and Ernest Twining endeavoured in his design to mitigate its abrasive effects by fitting oil seals to the motion wherever possible. Built in 1963 by Trevor Guest, *Siân* is a large 15in gauge engine and makes no pretence of being a miniature outline of a standard gauge locomotive. Twining piston valves are fitted, compressed air brakes operate on the tender and steam brakes on the engine. The engine was photographed at Ferry station on 12 October 1980 with Barmouth swing bridge in the background. (*Author*)

Above: Henry Greenly's initial post-first world war miniature railway assignment was the design and construction of the 15in gauge line at Dreamland Park, Margate. It was to be the last line Greenly was to design on the pre-war Miniature Railways Ltd model. Work began in March 1920, and the 600yd circuit around the perimeter of the park was opened during the summer. Due to the scarcity of timber after the war, the buildings were constructed of concrete but the two overbridges were built of steel. Motive power for the line came from Rhyl where Albert Barnes was building the first Atlantic of a type designed by Greenly at Barnes' request before the war. *Joan* entered service at Rhyl in 1920 which presumably enabled him to sell Little Giant No 15 *Prince Edward of Wales* (formerly *Red Dragon* while running on the White City Railway) to Margate. Six Bassett-Lowke four-wheel coaches were also supplied by Rhyl and rebuilt as an articulated set. When the park was redeveloped in 1924, the route of the line was changed into an end-to-end run of about $\frac{1}{4}$ mile. Unusually for a miniature railway, a traverser for engine release was provided at the main station. In 1928 Barnes supplied the fourth of his Greenly-designed Atlantics, No 104 *Billie*, to Margate where she ran until the end of 1979. *Billie* is seen here at Park station on 6 August 1979. She is now owned by a Rhyl businessman who is endeavouring to unite for the first time Barnes' six Atlantics on the Rhyl Miniature Railway. *Prince Edward of Wales* is now owned by W. H. McAlpine and Robin Butterell. (*P. H. Groom*)

As the most grandiose and elaborate miniature railway in the world, the Romney, Hythe & Dymchurch Railway merits above average space in any book on the subject, even though its history is well documented. The railway should have had two progenitors, Captain J. E. P. Howey and Count Louis Zborowski, but the latter was killed while driving in the Italian Grand Prix at Monza. There is strong evidence that the two men were *not* planning a railway of the size of the RH&DR when Zborowski was killed, but it was he who ordered what became the railway's first two engines, and there is little doubt that he would have taken a formative role in a new railway had he lived. In early 1925 Captain Howey began looking for a suitable site, his first preference being to buy the Ravenglass & Eskdale Railway and extend it to Ambleside. A more hare-brained scheme would be difficult to conceive, for it would have entailed taking the railway over the Hard Knott and Wrynose passes which with 1 in 3 hairpin climbs are taxing enough for cars. In the event, Howey's new railway was built through terrain that could be regarded as the antithesis of the Lake District — the flat land of Romney Marsh. Henry Greenly became involved with the scheme as engineer, and Sir Herbert Walker, General Manager of the Southern Railway, appears to have suggested the Romney area. One commercial virtue of the line was that it would connect two branches of the Southern, the terminus of the branch to New Romney, and Hythe on the Sandgate branch (cut back to Hythe in 1931). Preparatory work and the planning hurdles were tackled in earnest from September 1925, although Greenly and Howey regarded the latter somewhat lightly in the first instance. Construction began in 1926 and on 5 August 1926 the

railway was honoured by a visit from the Duke of York who travelled with Captain Howey on the footplate of No 2 *Northern Chief*. Nigel Gresley, whose Great Northern Pacifics had inspired Greenly's design, rode on the tender. The railway was formally opened from New Romney to Hythe on 16 July 1927, although special trains had already been running children to the Duke of York's holiday camp at Jesson

Top left: This was the layout at the throat of New Romney station before the line was extended to Dungeness on Bank Holiday weekend in August 1928. On the left is the paint shop and beyond is Carriage Depot No 1 which was superseded in 1928–9 by a larger shed alongside the station. The main line to Hythe may be seen to the right of the carriage shed, with the engine shed beyond. The paint shop was removed and the materials incorporated in the new carriage shed. (*L&GRP*)

THE ROMNEY, HYTHE & DYMCHURCH RAILWAY

Bottom left: Although Davey Paxman of Colchester were contracted to build the first eight locomotives, a company capable of producing miniature engines and of which Howey and Greenly were directors occupied the workshops at New Romney from their construction to 1928. Jackson, Rigby Ltd, which had operated at Shalford in Surrey, moved to New Romney while engaged in building two Greenly-designed 12in gauge American-type Pacifics for an exhibition line in Philadelphia. The purpose of the move was to enable the company to construct and repair various types of equipment, including signalling, for the RH&DR, while continuing its outside model engineering contracts and provision of a range of standard products. This dual purpose created such difficulties that Howey bought out the other shareholders so that the company's facilities could be devoted totally to the railway. This photograph was taken in 1927, before the line to No 1 road bypassed the turntable, showing the workshops on the right. Howey's house, Red Tiles, was to the right of the photograph. The layout of the shed roads was altered during the winter of 1936–7 when the turntable from Pilton Works on the Lynton & Barnstaple Railway was installed in its present position directly in front of the workshops. (*L&GRP*)

Above: Greenly's design for Howey and Zborowski was the culmination of 20 years' experience of locomotive design. He had acknowledged the advantages of overscale engines in his design for Albert Barnes, working to $\frac{1}{3}$ scale rather than $\frac{1}{4}$. Howey and Greenly admired Nigel Gresley's work and agreed to base the new design upon Gresley's A1 Pacific, the first of which had appeared in 1922. The standard of Davey Paxman's workmanship on the engines was regarded as being high, and the design was largely successful, the coil springs and gridiron superheater being the only two weaknesses. The coil springs, particularly those on the radial axles, caused bad rolling at speed. No 3 *Southern Maid* is seen here on the turntable at Hythe on 27 September 1930, showing the original type of tender. No 3 was photographed at Paxman's works with the name *Southern Chief*, but Howey changed his mind and the plates were removed before entering service. (*H. C. Casserley*)

Top right: Pacifics are not ideal locomotives for construction trains, whatever the gauge. Having learnt this the hard way, by frequent re-railings of Nos 1 and 2, a more suitable engine in the shape of an 0-4-0 tender tank from Krauss of Munich was ordered in 1926 by Jackson, Rigby Ltd (see page 37). Since the engine was urgently required, a standard 600mm gauge design by Roland Martens was adapted and delivered in May 1926. A side and well tank locomotive, *The Bug* was fitted with Stephenson's link motion and hand brakes only. Once her role as a contractor's locomotive ended, her utility was clearly in question since the need for a regular yard pilot at New Romney never developed. Accordingly she was sold in the early 1930s to a Blackpool showman and again in 1934, to Haymarket Amusements for use on the Bellevue Miniature Railway, situated in the park of that name five miles east of Belfast. At least two other 15in 0-4-0TT were built by Krauss: in 1927 the line at the Munich Exhibition centre was re-opened and two engines were required to replace the two Krauss Pacifics which had worked the line in 1925; Martens' 0-4-0TT design was

chosen and two were built and finished in Midland red with scarlet underframes. Their fate is not known but one went to Stuttgart after the exhibition closed where she was named *Schwarzer Otto*. (*W. A. Camwell collection*)

Bottom right: The Bellevue Miniature Railway was a single, straight track of about 200yd which operated from Easter to September. The three open bogie coaches and *The Bug*, renamed *Jean*, were kept in a wooden shed. About 1937, *Jean* was close to being renamed *Sir Crawford McCullagh* in honour of the then Lord Mayor of Belfast. On one occasion, in 1954, an on-site symposium of local model engineers and the owner's agent was convened to investigate the reason for *Jean*'s poor steaming. After the smokebox door had been opened, a 2lb hammer was requested and a couple of thwacks administered – the blastpipe had been knocked off centre and was delivering the exhaust against one edge of the chimney. When Barry's Amusements took over the line in 1959, plans for extending the Peter Pan Railway were made but a fire in the storage shed sealed the railway's fate and in 1960 *Jean* ended up in a Belfast scrap yard. There she remained until rescued by W. H. McAlpine in 1972. *Jean* was given a new boiler and tender and a thorough rebuild before being returned to service on the RH&DR as *The Bug*. Although not showing the whole engine, this photograph of *Jean* has been included for its rarity. (*Ulster Folk and Transport Museum*)

When planning the RH&DR, it was confidently expected that the railway would carry general merchandise, fish, coal and ballast. For this traffic, Greenly designed a 4-8-2 of similar appearance to the Pacifics but with a slightly longer boiler and coupled wheels of $19\frac{1}{2}$in as opposed to the $25\frac{1}{2}$in of the Pacifics. Two 4-8-2s were ordered, at the same time as Pacifics 7 and 8, and No 5 *Hercules* had the honour of hauling the official opening train. The goods traffic, however, failed to materialise: in one year only, 1929, was a respectable figure achieved when 891 tons was carried, largely due to War Department work near Maddieson's Camp. In 1932 the total slumped to 110tons. Moreover, the 4-8-2s were hard on the curves and the radius of certain points was less than desirable for the wheelbase. A pair of scissors crossovers at Hythe and New Romney were of such short radius that even the Pacifics protested; they were replaced by larger radius crossovers but the single points remained. Accordingly the two 4-8-2s were withdrawn from service when Nos 9 and 10 were delivered in 1931. In 1936 *Hercules* was rebuilt to work ballast trains and during the war was clad in steel plate for use on the armoured train which patrolled the line. *Hercules* is seen here on the turntable at Hythe on 28 August 1974. (*P. H. Groom*)

Right:
No 6 *Samson* waits to leave New Romney for Hythe on 19 August 1980. After her withdrawal from service in 1931, *Samson* was used as a source of spares for other engines, reducing her to a boiler shell and frames without wheels. In 1946–7 it was rebuilt in Hove and returned to service for the ballast traffic arising from the formation by some RH&DR directors of the Romney Marsh Ballast Co. *Hercules* was overhauled at the same time, at Ashford. The traffic was fraught with problems: a steep gradient between the pits near Maddieson's Camp and the main line, difficulties resulting from the shingle freezing in the skips, the economics of the operation were questionable and at least one major accident occurred when skips were strewn over both running lines at St Mary's Bay. In 1951 the traffic ceased, but the small radius points which had discouraged use of the 4-8-2s on service trains had gradually been replaced and accordingly both engines have since been in regular passenger use. (*P. H. Groom*)

Overleaf: What became RH&DR No 1 *Green Goddess* and No 2 *Northern Chief* were ordered by Count Zborowski, presumably for the line he was building at his home in Higham near Canterbury. *Green Goddess* was named after a play by William Archer which received its first performance in 1923; Howey obviously thought highly of it. Both engines were designed so that they could be converted to oil-firing, a tube for the fuel lead to the burner passing through the rear walls of the firebox underneath the door: they remained until both engines had their fireboxes patched in 1946. On completion by Davey Paxman in 1925, *Green Goddess* went to Ravenglass for ten days of trials. She performed to the satisfaction of all, achieving 35mph without effort and hauling 20 coaches (160 passengers) at an average speed of $22\frac{1}{2}$mph between Irton Road and Walkmill. The last part of the trials was to determine whether the vacuum or compressed air brake should be used. In due course the former was chosen and the Westinghouse pump used initially, which was mounted between the two rear splashers on the left-hand side, removed. *Green Goddess* was George Barlow's engine for over 30 years until his retirement as operating manager in 1981. No 1 has always been finished in green livery, the shade varying between LNER and GNR shades over the years. *Green Goddess* is seen here leaving Hythe with the 11.20am departure on 30 May 1980. (*P. H. Groom*)

Above: No 8 *Hurricane* was the last of the GN Pacifics to be delivered, on 20 July 1927. Like No 7 *Typhoon*, *Hurricane* was built as a three-cylinder engine and is seen here in New Romney shed in 1927. *Hurricane* and *Typhoon* were the outcome of Howey's desire to have a couple of really powerful engines. Greenly obliged by fitting a third cylinder of identical size to the outside pair, operated by Greenly's own design of radial valve gear. *Hurricane* became Howey's favourite engine, being the first engine to be given a high capacity tender, in 1934, and having stainless steel handrails. *Typhoon* was converted to a two-cylinder engine by Davey Paxman in 1935–6, but *Hurricane* retained her third cylinder until she failed in traffic in July 1937. For a week, a man from Davey Paxman tinkered with the jammed motion until Howey ordered the third cylinder to be blanked off; it was not finally removed until the engine was rebuilt during 1972–3. Howey lost interest in the engine and it was renamed *Bluebottle* in 1938 after being given a coat of blue paint (over LNER green) in readiness for The Blue Train. This was an express service, using ten blue saloons. (*L&GRP*)

Top right: No 10 *Dr Syn* leaves Dymchurch with the 11.24am from New Romney to Hythe on 6 September 1980. No 10 was originally named *Black Prince*, receiving her present name from No 9 when the latter went to Toronto as *Winston Churchill* in 1948. As built and delivered, the boilers of both engines were set at 200lb/sq in whereas Martens/Krauss had recommended 171lb/sq in. The collapse of a steam pipe in about 1935 prompted their reduction to 180lb/sq in. During the war No 10 had the misfortune to fall into a bomb crater, and by 1945 was in a semi-dismantled state. It was rebuilt at New Romney during the winter of 1946–7. Both Nos 9 and 10 were originally finished in black with blued-steel boiler cladding. *Winston Churchill* has been painted in a bright red for most of the post-war years, while *Dr Syn* has been black apart from 11 years in Great Western green. (*P. H. Groom*)

Bottom right: The last two locomotives built for the RH&DR were very different from their predecessors, being based on the light Pacifics of the Canadian National Railways. The two engines were needed because of the additional trains being operated after the full opening of the Dungeness extension in 1928. An order for two more LNER-type Pacifics was placed with Davey Paxman but this was cancelled when Howey decided to have a Canadian outline engine. Their genesis is confused but it is certain that the boilers were designed by Roland Martens of Krauss and built by that company. It was originally intended that the engines would be assembled by Jackson, Rigby at New Romney but the task was given to the Yorkshire Engine Company, using some parts that had been made at New Romney and Colchester. No 9 *Doctor Syn*, named after the famous fictional smuggling parson of Dymchurch, was the first of the two engines. Both were originally fitted with Vanderbilt tenders which incorporated vacuum-operated water scoops – at the time there was a scheme to install water troughs near Greatstone. The Vanderbilt tenders were prone to leakage and No 9 was given a conventional tender built on the original wheels and frames of No 10's tender in 1962. In September 1948 No 9 was renamed *Winston Churchill* before going to Toronto for an exhibition; the name *Dr Syn* was given to No 10 in February 1949. No 9 is seen here at New Romney with its Vanderbilt tender. (*L&GRP*)

No 3 *Southern Maid* is seen here crossing New Dyke on 5 July 1976. She has been through more changes of livery than any other engine on the railway: originally finished in LNER green, the army repainted her during the war in 'Wickham blue' (not unlike Caledonian blue), since when she has been turned out in green, LB&SCR Marsh umber, French grey, Malachite green, and GN green with dark green border and brown frames. (*P. H. Groom*)

No 6 *Samson* near the Warren with the 10.20am from
Hythe on 28 August 1979. *Samson's* livery was originally
LNER apple green. She was finished in Malachite green
from 1947 to 1955, since when she has been painted
black with the lining that adorned Caledonian Railway
mixed traffic engines. (*P. H. Groom*)

No 7 *Typhoon* was the first of the two three-cylinder Pacifics, being delivered in May 1927, two months before *Hurricane*. *Typhoon* lost her third cylinder two years before her sister, being sent to Davey Paxman for rebuilding in 1936–7. The third cylinder and steam chest were left *in situ*. In 1965 a pair of Gresham & Craven ejectors were fitted just forward of the cab on the left-hand side, covered by a streamlined casing. *Typhoon* is seen here approaching Dungeness with the 11.20am from Hythe on 6 September 1980. (*P. H. Groom*)

Above: In 1937 six engines with a resemblance to the DB 01 Pacifics were built, three by Krupp for the Gruga Park in Essen, and three by Krauss of Munich for an exhibition line in Dresden. The latter engines went to Cologne in 1939 and escaped damage during the war by being stored several miles out of the city. They were restored in 1961 for use at the Bundesgartenshau in Cologne. Afterwards they were returned to store until purchased for a new amusement park on the banks of the Rhine north of Cologne. The engines were never used for want of skilled labour and because of objections to the idea of smoke. In 1972 Alan Bloom was able to purchase two of them for a new 15in gauge line which was planned to replace the $10\frac{1}{4}$ in gauge line at Bressingham Gardens, Diss, Norfolk. Little mechanical work was required; the Prussian blue was replaced by Brunswick green and the engines were given their former names, *Rosenkavalier* and *Männertrau*.

The third engine, *Fleissig Lieschen*, was retained by the owner for sentimental reasons, but in 1976 the RH&DR was able to purchase it. The engine was given the number 11, renamed *Black Prince* (the name of No 10 until 1949) and finished in black and red. *Rosenkavalier* visited the RH&DR in 1980 and is seen here waiting to leave Hythe with *Black Prince* on 5 October. (*P. H. Groom*)

Below: The cab layout and the robustness of the controls give the appearance of being scaled-down reproductions of the full-size engines. In the smaller scales, gauges, lack of space and the reduced dimensions of pipe work, with correspondingly finer controls, require an approach which rules out considerations about the layout and appearance of the prototype. This is the cab of No 2 *Northern Chief*, taken in 1970, still with Greenly tender. (*G. M. Kichenside*)

Above: The first miniature railway at Southsea was a 9½in gauge line opened in 1924 by the corporation with a Bassett-Lowke Great Northern Atlantic seen here. The line ran for about ¾ mile with a balloon loop at one end and run round at the other. After the war, the line was revived by Southern Miniature Railways Ltd on almost the same route but in 10¼in gauge. A freelance 4-4-2 1002 *Valiant* commenced services and was joined in 1948 by another Atlantic 1003 *Victory*, built by SMR and similar to *Vanguard* at Poole. (*C. M. Whitehouse collection*)

Below: The Downs Light Railway was conceived by Geoffrey Hoyland, headmaster of The Downs School, as a hobby and teaching exercise for the boys who have always spent one afternoon a week on one of a range of pursuits.

BETWEEN THE WARS

An engine was acquired before much thought had been given to the railway itself: built by a Mr Spriggs of Birmingham between 1908–12, *Tubby* was a freelance 7¼in 2-6-2 with a Goodhand boiler, Joy valve gear, outside frames and a Great Western air to her. The gauge of the railway was therefore pre-determined, and construction proceeded in 1925, entailing considerable earthworks including a curved 25yd tunnel under a road. *Tubby* is seen here in May 1928 before it was sent to R. N. Morse of Brighton for the valve gear to be changed and a parallel boiler to be fitted. In 1936–7, the gauge was changed because Geoffrey Hoyland had bought a 9½in gauge engine, an LBSC Stroudley 0-4-2T *Ranmore* built by Morse. *Tubby* was regauged, and in 1941 was joined by *George*, a GN Atlantic built about 1932 by Bullock using some Bassett-Lowke parts. This private railway is currently undergoing a renascence under the direction of J. I. C. Boyd. (*R. H. Webster*)

Above: Owned by Alex Schwab, the $7\frac{1}{4}$in gauge Saltwood Miniature Railway near Hythe in Kent was begun in 1924 following a move from its former location in Sheffield. The 610ft oval has a 36ft brick-lined tunnel and has been open to the public regularly since 1931, all revenue being donated to charities. The Atlantic *Trojan* was originally an unnamed 0-4-2T built by Jubb Ltd of Sheffield with the unusual feature of hard steel tyres shrunk onto cast-iron wheels. In 1928, while the line was being relaid with 9lb/yd rail, the engine was rebuilt as a 4-4-2 with a semi-flash boiler. This did not prove a success and it was replaced by a Goodhand copper boiler. This photograph of *Trojan* at the only station must have been taken between 1929–33: the Siphon van behind the engine was built in 1929, using the line's original bogie carriage as a basis, to distance passengers from the rather wet exhaust of *Trojan*; in 1933 with a need for more capacity it was rebuilt to carry three people. (*Alex Schwab collection*)

Below: The Saltwood Miniature Railway's second steam engine was the 2-6-0 *Maid of Kent*, designed by Greenly from Alex Schwab's basic concept. With a Great Western outline, Walschaert's valve gear excepted, the engine was a great success and relegated *Trojan* to second engine until both were withdrawn in 1970 and subsequently sold. *Maid of Kent* was rebuilt as a Southern U class Mogul and now runs on the Great Cockrow Railway as No 1803 *River Itchen*. At least two other Greenly GW Moguls survive, one on the line in Wellington Country Park between Reading and Basingstoke. The Saltwood line is now operated by a pair of electric locomotives, one with the unusual miniature feature of a double cab with drive facility at each end. *Great Western* is seen here with the only enclosed carriage on the railway at the end of the train. This carriage was once a diesel locomotive which ran on a garden railway at Lechlade. (*J. C. Adams*)

Left: In 1929 Colonel R. B. Tyrrell bought Henry Greenly's bungalow at New Romney following Greenly's departure after the dispute with the RH&DR over a supposedly missing drawing. This episode led to a court case in which Greenly was granted an absolute discharge with costs. Col Tyrrell was introduced to Howey who granted him a strip of land on which to lay a 600yd 7½in gauge line. It was built to 7½in gauge, as opposed to 7¼in, because Col Tyrrell logically argued that 1½in scale should have exactly half the gauge of 3in scale (15in gauge). West Coast Americans also use 7½in gauge but in the East and in Britain we may agree, but do not act upon it! The first engine to operate the New Romney Miniature Railway was a 4-4-0, based loosely on a London & South Western Railway T3 4-4-0 which Col Tyrrell had built during service in Malta. This locomotive proved inadequate and Col Tyrrell designed and built in the RH&DR workshops an 0-4-4T *Atlanta* which hauled the six oak-framed bogie carriages with ease. The line closed during the war and afterwards was converted to 10¼in at Howey's suggestion. *Atlanta* operated for a few years on the Folkestone Miniature Railway which Col Tyrrell operated for a few seasons. (*Dr J. Hollick collection*)

Bottom left: The 15in gauge Porthcawl Miniature Railway was opened in 1932, running for 400yd to Coney Beach. A loop was provided at the midway point and a tunnel built to double as an engine shed. The first engine was 4-6-4T *Coney Queen*, designed largely by Sir Leslie Joseph and built by a small firm of engineers at Pengam, Cardiff. It was powered by a 12hp four-cylinder Austin petrol engine transmitting power through an infinitely variable Vickers hydraulic gear, concocted from two fin controls of a submarine being scrapped at Newport. The concealed radiator was so arranged that the water frequently boiled to give off a whiff of steam. In 1935 a slightly larger engine, *Silver Jubilee*, was built by the same firm using a 16hp Austin engine with power transmitted by an electric generator and motor taken from a Tillings Stephens bus. The final drive was by an external chain to the rear driving axle. Both engines are still running on the railway although *Coney Queen*, seen here before the war, has been converted to petrol-electric because of the non-availability of parts for the Vickers hydraulics. The 12 coaches came from the Romney, Hythe & Dymchurch Railway. (*Courtesy Sir Leslie Joseph*)

Below: The impressive Farnborough Green terminus of the remarkable Surrey Border & Camberley Railway, photographed in June 1939. In the photograph are a Garratt 2-6-6-2T and a Pacific. But what gauge? See over. (*L&GRP*)

The Surrey Border & Camberley Railway was one of the most elaborate 10¼in gauge lines ever built. At its greatest extent the route length was 2¼ miles. It began life as the Foxhill Miniature Railway, construction beginning in late 1934 by H. C. S. Bullock, the well-known locomotive builder who then lived at Farnborough. Running from Foxhill station, where there was an island platform, engine shed, turntable and signal box, the line passed through fields and woodland to Lye Copse station which was provided with two platforms and a run-round loop. In early 1936, the co-ownership of the railway was obtained by a merchant banker, Alexander Davenport Kinloch, and improvements were made with a view to opening the railway to the public, on 23 May 1936. After Bullock's death in 1937, Kinloch extended the line to Hawley, creating a large radius circle for turning trains, on which there were also a terminal platform and run-round loop, and made further improvements such as the erection of an overall roof at Foxhill. Despite extensive advertising and the carrying of 35,000 passengers between May and September 1937, the line made an operating loss. The only way to increase traffic was considered to be an extension which would take the line alongside a main road to attract passing motorists. Accordingly the Surrey Border & Camberley Railway was formed to purchase the assets of the Farnborough Miniature Railway (as it had been renamed in 1937) and construct a new line from Camberley to Farnborough Green at Frimley Bridge. The latter was situated on the main London – Aldershot road, and a branch line to Blackwater, which never materialised, was planned to tap the London – Southampton road. The Southern Railway station at Frimley was 200yd from Farnborough Green station and through tickets over the SB&CR were obtainable at main stations such as Waterloo, Ascot, Reading, Guildford and Woking. The new line was opened on 23 July 1938 by the actor Graham Moffat of *Oh Mr Porter* and other Will Hay comedies.

Below: In his capacity as a merchant banker Kinloch was involved with the Leeds firm of locomotive builders Kitson & Co. As a result, a Kitson director, H. M. Gulland, became a director of the SB&CR and Kitsons was given an order in 1938 for two 2-6-6-2 Garratt locomotives, the only miniature or Garratt locomotives ever to be built by the company. Both engines were delivered later that year. They were powerful machines, rated at 28hp and capable of pulling 120 passengers, but problems were experienced with derailments, thought to be caused by the way the leading axle was fixed to the frames. No 4012 was sold to Charles Lane to run on his Royal Anchor Railway at Liphook in Hampshire, which opened about 1948. For some time the engine was at Beyer Peacock's works in Manchester awaiting regauging, following the engine's sale to a Rhodesian. Beyer Peacock declined the task and No 4012 remained there until bought by Sir Thomas Salt. He had the engine rebuilt at the Cambrian Railways' works in Oswestry with taller chimney, cab and dome giving the engine a narrow gauge appearance. Charles Simpson designed the modifications. Salt's intention was to use it on the railway round his pig farm at Shillingstone in Dorset. Unfortunately his death while the work was being carried out at Oswestry prevented this although the engine was delivered to Shillingstone. It is now on a plinth in Wimborne. (*L&GRP*)

Above: Cove Wood station was the first stop after leaving Farnborough Green and the venue for seasonal junketings organised by the railway, such as firework parties and the distribution of presents by Father Christmas. The line from Farnborough Green was double track as far as Cove Wood and single thereafter. The engine is 0-4-2/0-6-0T No 3008, a freelance design which was built in 1934 for the FMR by Bullock and worked for a time at California in England, Berkshire. It is thought that it was rebuilt as an 0-6-0T but whether this was the case at all, and if so, whether it was done at Farnborough or at Severn Beach where it subsequently went, remains one of the many enigmas which surround most of the SB&CR engines. (*L&GRP*)

Below: Camberley station with No 2006 *King Edward VIII.* Built in 1934 for Mr Cookson of Horsham, No 2006 was a freelance Pacific of Great Western outline and was the only engine to work on the FMR and SB&CR from 1935 to 1939. Camberley station was provided with a single platform, a substantial booking office and signalbox. The main engine shed and workshops, together with carriage sidings, were also built adjacent to a residential area. Unlike Farnborough Green, the station was never completed due to the outbreak of war. (*H. C. Casserley*)

Above: Garratt No 4012 leaving Farnborough Green. The line was fully signalled, the box on the right having 40 levers. The line immediately on the photographer's side of the box led to a three-road engine shed, while the nearer line ran to a turntable. Behind the signal and engine is the railway-owned tearoom. The articulated coaches are worthy of note. (*L&GRP*)

Right upper: Emerging from Cove Wood on the double track section between Farnborough Green and Cove Wood. There have been few miniature railways with such a long section of double track, while the good reproductions of signals and telegraph poles all helped to give a full-size atmosphere to the railway. (*H. C. Casserley*)

Right: The identity of this engine crossing the River Blackwater near Cove Wood station is unrecorded but it is thought to be Bullock Pacific No 1003 *Western Queen*, built in 1934, after reboilering in 1938. The photograph is dated June 1939. One of the attractions of the SB&CR was the opportunity to 'drive the engine yourself'. For this privilege, 10 shillings (50p) was charged for the full run, compared with 1s 6d (15p) for a normal single from Farnborough Green to Camberley. Sadly the line closed on the outbreak of the second world war and by the end of hostilities, the stock had been dispersed or scrapped and some of the buildings dismantled. (*L&GRP*)

Above: W. L. Jennings was responsible for the construction of two public miniature railways and several garden lines, all in 9½in gauge. His first public railway was at Weymouth where this photograph of Jennings (centre) and his Baltimore & Ohio Railroad A3 Atlantic No 1430 *Lake Shore* was taken. *Lake Shore*, fitted with Baker valve gear, began its life at Weymouth, moving to Crowthorne Farm (Berkshire), Danson Park and Brooklands before being converted to 10¼in gauge. The line at Weymouth was a 400yd oval on the sea front and was built between 1934–6. The second public line was at Barry Island where it ran round a boating lake. A dining car with table lamps in which teas were served and even a closed sleeping car were provided — Sir Arthur would have approved. (*John Hall-Craggs collection*)

Top right: The 20in gauge North Bay Railway at Scarborough was built by the Borough Council and opened in 1931. The single line runs for almost a mile through Northstead Manor Gardens and above the beach at North Bay. The line is controlled by a key system which was installed by the Railway Signal Company of Liverpool in 1933, following an accident in the previous year which claimed a driver's life. A passing loop at the now closed Beach station permits a two-train service. In 1948 a system was introduced whereby ramps activated the compressed air brakes on the carriages if the single line keys were not in the correct position. Originally the line had no functional signals but in 1977 colour light signals and barriers were installed at Scalby Mills, the main station. The line is one of the most heavily used in the country, with over ½ million passengers in a season on record. (*Graham Ellis collection*)

Right: The North Bay Railway has two locomotives, numbered 1931 and 1932 to denote the year of their construction, and named *Neptune* and *Triton* respectively. Based on Gresley's A3 Pacifics, they were built by Hudswell Clarke of Leeds and originally fitted with 32hp Dorman engines. Now powered by Perkins 43hp engines, they have a torque converter which eliminates gears and clutch, and makes very smooth starts possible. Operation of the converter is similar to a turbine, with no wearing parts and filled with water and a small quantity of cooledge compound. The speed is governed entirely by the revolutions of the engine. A worm and pinion final drive is fitted to the middle pair of driving wheels. The fuel tank is positioned in the firebox and holds 5 gallons of gas oil. Sanding gear is fitted to the leading and trailing driving wheels. *Neptune* is seen here with a well-filled train at Scalby Mills in the 1930s. (*Graham Ellis collection*)

Above: Soon after the North Bay Railway at Scarborough was opened, Hudswell Clarke & Co built two more steam outline diesel engines for a new line at Blackpool Pleasure Beach which opened in 1934. Running through the fairground, the 1200yd, 21in gauge line incorporated a wooden replica of the Forth Bridge spanning an ornamental lake. A3 Pacific 4472 *Mary Louise* and freelance 4-6-4T *Carol Jean*, seen here with the Big Dipper in the background, were built in 1933, and followed the construction of two identical engines, but to 20in gauge, for a line at Golden Acre Park in Leeds. A3 *May Thompson* and 4-6-4T *Robin Hood* were later bought by the owners of the Blackpool line and used, together with the track from Golden Acre Park, to establish the 500yd Morecambe Miniature Railway in April 1953. (*Graham Ellis collection*)

Below: In 1938 a ½ mile, 21in gauge railway was constructed at Bellahouston Park, Glasgow, in conjunction with the British Empire Exhibition. Two internal combustion powered engines, *Princess Elizabeth* and *Princess Margaret Rose*, based on the Stanier Pacifics of the same names, were built for the occasion by Hudswell Clarke. *Princess Margaret Rose* was finished in LNER livery with 'Clacton Express' above the smokebox door and *Princess Elizabeth*, seen here at the exhibition, was painted in LMS livery with 'Skegness Special' over the smokebox door, in both cases indicating their destinations after the exhibition. Both lines were operated at the Butlins Holiday Camps. *Princess Margaret Rose* was later renamed *Queen Elizabeth* and ran at Pwllheli while *Princess Elizabeth* subsequently went to Minehead. Henry Greenly and his wife made one of their rare forays

north of the border for the exhibition, taking a coastal steamer from London to Dundee and touring the Highlands before coming south to Glasgow. Greenly had been to the Glasgow Exhibition before, in 1901 for the very first such occasion when a Cagney 4-4-0 was hauling visitors round the grounds. Percival Marshall, founder and editor of *The Model Engineer*, accompanied Greenly. (*H. C. Casserley*)

Above: Scotland has few public miniature railways. The oldest and best known is Kerr's Miniature Railway which runs for 400yd beside the East Coast Main Line at Arbroath in Angus. The line opened in 1935 on $7\frac{1}{4}$in gauge with a freelance Atlantic built by Lewis Shaw of Ilkeston. The heavy traffic prompted a change of gauge in 1937; today a more powerful engine would have been acquired but the state of miniature locomotive design at the time made an increase to $10\frac{1}{4}$in gauge the optimum solution. The first $10\frac{1}{4}$in engine was also the first locomotive to have been built by H. C. S. Bullock — a freelance 4-4-0 of Great Western outline, which had previously worked at California-in-England. The engine was known as *Gladstone* but it is thought that nameplates were not fitted. This photograph shows *Auld Reekie*, a freelance Atlantic based upon an LNER C6, which is powered by a 1924 Austin 7 petrol engine. The engine was built by W. L. Jennings in 1938 for the $9\frac{1}{2}$in gauge Barry Island Miniature Railway, arriving at Arbroath in 1945. Although semi-retired, *Auld Reekie*'s original petrol engine has been recently overhauled by the local vintage car club. On the right is Bullock Pacific *King George VI* which was built about 1936 as *Silver Jubilee* for Mr Cookson of Horsham. It worked at Bramber Castle in 1936 and moved to the Surrey Border & Camberley Railway in 1937–8 from where it was purchased by Matthew Kerr. In 1960 it was sold to a haulage contractor in the Midlands for £350 and subsequently found its way to Hayling Island. Since 1960, Kerr's Miniature Railway has been worked by internal combustion engines, but in 1981 steam returned in the form of LMS Class 5 *Ayrshire Yeomanry* which was en route to Mull. In the background is full size Class A2 Pacific No 60528 *Tudor Minstrel*. (*J. B. White Ltd*)

When W. G. Bagnall Ltd of Stafford built in 1893 an 18in gauge Great Northern Stirling Single for the Marquis of Downshire, they also made a second set of castings which eventually went to the Regent Street Polytechnic in 1898. Henry Greenly was then attending evening classes at the Polytechnic and assisted with the construction of No 1. The engine was on exhibition at the Polytechnic for a time and was rebuilt by a Mr Notter of the GNR Locomotive Department before he sold it to the Fairbourne Railway. The FR needed a second engine to enable repairs to be carried out on *Count Louis* but the decision to buy No 1 was extraordinary, not least because it was of a different gauge from the Fairbourne 15in track. This impediment was overcome by laying a third rail but the Single was quite unsuitable for the loadings and was sold in 1936 to Miniature Railway & Special Engineering of Eastbourne. This concern had been given the task of establishing a railway by F. C. Stedman of Clacton. The Jaywick Miniature Railway, situated in a developing holiday area near Clacton, was opened on 31 July 1936 by C. H. Newton, Divisional Manager of the LNER, who may be seen holding the flag in this photograph of the opening. (*Left*) The 18in gauge, one mile line began at Jaywick Sands station and ran to Cross Ways, passing through a 60ft tunnel driven through a pre-historic barrow. The line had many sharp curves which caused slipping in wet weather. No 1 had a compressed air brake pump fitted on the right-hand side of the cab to operate the tender brakes, a hand brake being used on the engine. (*Below*) Soon after

opening, a driver's error caused the engine to overrun the stop block which resulted in the loss of the front left-hand buffer. Trouble with the boiler due to poor local water encouraged the construction of a oil-fired Sentinel with a water tube boiler of Lune Valley type to replace No 1. Steam could be raised in eight minutes from cold. The three eight-seat, 18ft coaches on the line were built by Caffyn of Eastbourne in 1936 and were unusually well appointed. Built of ash frames and steel underframes, they were painted bright green with cream roofs and provided with electric lights. When the railway closed with the beginning of the second world war, the coaches and the Sentinel were sold to the New Brighton Railway. From there the coaches went in 1965 to the Ravenglass & Eskdale Railway which had, of course, to regauge them. In 1976 they were again sold, to the Narrow Gauge Railway Centre at Gloddfa Ganol, Blaenau Ffestiniog. The subsequent history of No 1 is somewhat clouded but the engine still exists and is believed to be undergoing restoration. (*Clacton Library*)

THE LAST 30 YEARS
7¼in GAUGE EXPANDS

Right: One of the most elaborate and sophisticated 7¼in gauge systems is the Great Cockrow Railway near Chertsey in Surrey. Using equipment from the Greywood Central Railway at Walton on Thames, built by the late Sir John Samuel after the second world war, the railway provides a normal main line distance of 1,580yd with a branch line of 310yd. However, it is the thoroughness of the signalling system which impresses the first-time visitor. Although controlled from three signalboxes, the railway is fully signalled using a variety of former standard gauge power lever frames for mechanical signals and points, ex-LNWR three-position block instruments, Tyer's No 12A electric token instruments, scale GCR, LMS and colour-light signals, and track circuit diagrams, with manual double-line block, electric token single line, and track-circuit block operation. The semaphore signals are equipped with lights for night running which occurs on the first Saturday of November when Shepperton Rotary Club organises a bonfire night to raise money for charity. The main station and terminus of the line is Hardwick Central, where H. Saunders' superb LNER K3 2-6-0, built in 1975, is seen waiting to leave. (*Author*)

Left: LMS *Royal Scot* and NER R1 4-4-0 outside the seven-road shed at Hardwick Central on the Great Cockrow Railway. The *Royal Scot* was built in 1947 by Cecil Barnett and Len Willoughby, a locomotive inspector at Eastleigh, using Bassett-Lowke castings. The NER R1 was built as early as 1912 by Baldwin Brothers, later Models Ltd, and is one of the oldest $7\frac{1}{4}$in gauge engines still running. When purchased from the Lewisham area, where it had been running, it was found that the tender journals consisted of oak blocks with steel tube inserts! (*G. M. Kichenside*)

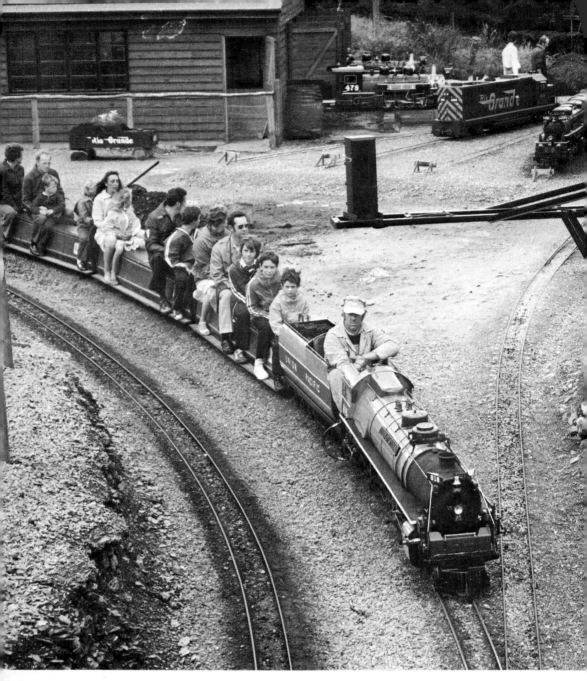

Above: One of the most extensive $7\frac{1}{4}$in gauge systems in the country is the Forest Railroad at Dobwalls near Liskeard in Cornwall. Two separate but interlaced lines, based on the Denver & Rio Grande and the Union Pacific railroads, give a total run of two miles on land that was once covered by a pig farm. Landscaping with conifers and American-style lineside buildings and artefacts give an authentic flavour to a journey behind one of John Southern's impressive American locomotives. In this view of Union Pacific 4-8-4 No 818 *Queen of Wyoming* passing the engine shed, all but one of the engines are visible – the two Rio Grande 2-8-2s, K36 No 488 *General Palmer* and K37 No 498 *Otto Mears*, both built by David Curwen, the Rio Grande Bo-Bo diesel *Mathias Baldwin*, Union Pacific 4-8-8-4 Big Boy No 4008 *William Jeffers*, and Union Pacific DD40X diesel No 6908 *Centennial*. Only David Curwen's 2-6-2, named after its builder, is missing. *Queen of Wyoming* built by Severn-Lamb and delivered in Spring 1974, is a model of one of the 4-8-4 Northerns introduced by UP in 1937. The 45 engines of the class were designed for continuous high-speed running, with roller bearings, and No 815 was the first locomotive ever to haul a 1,000 ton train at 100mph. (*Author*)

Below: The Severn-Lamb Big Boy shares with Coleby-Simkins' 10¼in gauge Berkshire and 7¼in gauge 59 Class Garratt the laurels for sophisticated miniature engineering. They will be joined by John Wilks' Niagara. These engines incorporate important developments, both in terms of the complexity of the equipment on the prototype which is reproduced in working order on the miniature engine, and the methods adopted in their construction. The Big Boy 4-8-8-4 No 4008 *William Jeffers* was delivered to the Forest Railroad in November 1978, ready for the opening of the Union Pacific route on 7 April 1979. Twenty-five of the full-size giants were built to haul 5,000 ton loads over the Wahsatch and Sherman hills of Wyoming. They were the largest and most powerful steam locomotives ever built. The Forest Railroad is perhaps unique in that it takes several journeys on each route for the visitor to familiarise himself with the layout, so intricately have the design and complementary landscaping been evolved. An outstanding collection of Thorburn's bird and wildlife paintings and a model railway are other attractions. (*Author*)

Left: The one-third scale 7¼in gauge Lynton & Barnstaple Railway 2-6-2T *Yeo* on the Riverside Miniature Railway at Buckfastleigh, Dart Valley Railway steam centre. *Yeo* was built by Milner Engineering who also built a second sister engine, *Taw*, for display in the entrance to the National Railway Museum. The main difference is the absence of footwells for the driver on *Taw*. The prototypes were fitted with Joy valve gear which has been faithfully reproduced by John Milner. *Yeo* is seen here crossing the bridge over the pond in the DVR station grounds. (*Author*)

Top right: As part of the attractions for the public at the factory of the model railway suppliers Peco at Beer near Seaton in Devon, a 7¼in gauge line of about ¼ mile has been built on the hillside above the factory. Opened by Rev W. Awdrey on 14 July 1975, the line affords spectacular views along the coast. No 4 *Thomas II* passes the engine shed with the first train of the day on 5 June 1980. *Thomas II* was built by Roger Marsh in 1979. The line descending to a lower level between the engine shed and the train terminates in a workshop with raised track level to facilitate work on the engines. The Beer Heights Light Railway is undoubtedly one of the most immaculately maintained lines in the country. The ballast looks almost as though it is regularly washed! Work has begun on extending the line to a new terminal station which will be reached by tunnelling the line under the car park behind Much Natter station. (*Author*)

Right: No 3 *Dickie*, built by David Curwen, is seen here leaving what must be one of the deepest cuttings on a miniature railway. The driver is Mr K. Beeley who used to operate the miniature railway at Glossop. The track and rolling stock were made by Cromar White. (*Peco*)

Above: One of the most sophisticated signalling systems in the country is to be found on the privately-run Spinney Light Railway. The 7¼in line is fully signalled with scale LNWR signals operated from three signalboxes; two of the boxes are fitted with Cromar White mechanical frames and the third with a miniature mechanical frame, two having electrical contacts. All points are worked from the boxes, mostly by windscreen wiper motors. The running lines are controlled by LNWR three-position block instruments and fully interlocked frames. Starting signals are interlocked with the instruments. The railway is operated according to the SLR rule book with which signalmen and drivers are expected to be conversant. The line is in the form of a ham bone with a triangular junction leading to a terminus. Here a Bassett-Lowke George the Fifth class 4-4-0 leaves Baytree Junction. In May 1911, the price for a 7¼in gauge ex-works George the Fifth was £110 with £5 15s extra for steam brakes. A GCR Immingham was £185. (*Author*)

Top right: Since the late 1960s there has been a growing effort to develop the potential of the miniature locomotive beyond what is required by the needs of a purely commercial operation. An example of this upsurge of creative engineering is the pair of oil-fired 7¼in gauge East African Railways 59 class Garratts built by Coleby-Simkins. The inspiration for their construction came from Brian Hollingsworth, who owns *Mount Kilimanjaro*, after seeing the metre gauge prototypes at work in Kenya. They are the most powerful metre gauge engines in the world and the 7¼in engines are contenders for the same distinction in the smaller gauge. The engines have four 3¾

x 5½in cylinders, a water tank capacity of 50 gallons and measure 19ft 6in over the couplers. Domestic central heating oil is used as fuel. Finished in EAR maroon livery, lined in black and yellow, *Mount Kilimanjaro* is seen here with Neil Simkins. (*J. B. Hollingsworth*)

Right: Even in Bassett-Lowke's works, it is very unlikely that six engines would have been under construction at any one time as seen here at Roger Marsh's Britannia Works in Leicestershire. The engines are Tinkerbells, an 0-4-2T design by Roger Marsh based on *Dot*, the 0-4-0 well tank built by Beyer Peacock in 1877 for shunting on the 18in gauge line round its works at Gorton in Manchester. In the foreground is a Hunslet 0-4-0ST belonging to Bob Jones which was in the works for repairs to a wheel flange following a collision with a caravan which had stopped on a level crossing. (*Roger Marsh*)

Overleaf: The 7¼in gauge line at the Conwy Valley Railway Museum, Betws-y-coed, was opened in May 1979. Running alongside the LNWR branch line to Blaenau Ffestiniog, the ½ mile line is in the shape of a ham bone with the station roughly midway along the parallel lines. The original *Romulus* and another of the same type *Bethany* share the traffic with a Hunslet 0-4-0ST. *Bethany* is seen here with Dr Brian Rogers in charge on 11 October 1980. The track has been fabricated from BR channel point rodding and trains are fitted with vacuum brakes. The museum contains a very fine collection of railway relics and some of the late Jack Nelson's beautifully made 3½mm scale dioramas of LNWR scenes. (*Author*)

Above: Broadly speaking, there are two, sometimes conflicting, considerations to apply to locomotive design in miniature gauges: the necessity of producing a practical, functional machine; and the desire to reproduce a scale model of a favoured full-size design. Most builders steer a middle course, compromising on points of detail in the interests of the first point. The difficulties that can arise from basing a design on a full-size prototype may be eased by choosing a freelance design in which the constraints naturally disappear. Or a larger scale, say one-third rather than quarter-scale, can be used to make for a more robust and functional engine. Many refuse to take either of these courses, or to simplify a standard-gauge design, their pleasure being to reproduce an engine as exactly as possible in the correct scale. Supreme examples of this are these two $7\frac{1}{4}$in gauge Castle class locomotives, *Winchester Castle* and *Monmouth Castle*, built by Keith Wilson of Devon, correct to the number of rivets. (*Keith Wilson*)

Top Right: The Hilton Valley Railway in Shropshire was created by Michael Lloyd and opened at Easter 1956. For 23 years the line carried up to 25,000 passengers a year,

even though it operated only on Sundays and Bank Holidays during the summer. In 1979 the house and the grounds through which the $\frac{3}{4}$ mile line ran were sold. A new site was found at Weston Park, home of the earls of Bradford and situated on the A5 near Shifnal. The seventeenth-century house has been open to the public for some years with a range of other attractions. The target was to dismantle the HVR after the service ended in September 1979, move all the track and stock to Weston Park and construct the new line in readiness for the 1980 opening at Easter. The objective was just achieved, the new line of over $\frac{2}{3}$ mile opening on 5 April 1980. The new line passes through part of the gardens at Weston Park and provides views of the lake and open country. Two of the four engines had been overhauled during the winter by Milner Engineering, the 4-8-4 No 3 *Francis Henry Lloyd* receiving a new boiler. No 3 was begun by Trevor Guest to Greenly's drawings of a Canadian prototype and completed by apprentices of F. H. Lloyd's training school in 1959. Baker valve gear and screw reverse were fitted. The most historic engine on the line is No 1 *Lorna Doone*, a Pacific built by Louis Shaw of Ilkeston in 1925 and used at Mablethorpe until 1939. (*Author*)

Right: The $10\frac{1}{4}$in gauge circuit at Tucktonia leisure park in Christchurch, built in 1973, was reopened on 1 April 1981 after conversion to $7\frac{1}{4}$in gauge by Narogauge Ltd. At the same time the track was extended to run along the River Stour, giving a ride of approximately $\frac{1}{2}$ mile. The new four-road shed, with space for a further two lines, may be seen in this photograph of *Tinkerbell* on the new section of line. Outside the shed are the two other Tinkerbells, *Talos* and *Medea*, the latter finished in LBSC Marsh umber livery. Most of the rolling stock, which includes a caboose, has been built largely by Jim Haylock. (*Author*)

THE MINIATURE RAILWAY. WEYMOUTH.
C.M.1187.

Top left: In June 1947 a 1100yd, $10\frac{1}{4}$in gauge line opened along the edge of Radipole Lake at Weymouth by David Curwen and the Baydon Miniature Railway Co. It had an LNER-type Pacific No 2001 *Robin Hood* fitted with Baker valve gear. No 2001 had a sister which went to Hillsea; they were Curwen's first engines. The proximity to the lake proved a mixed blessing on one occasion – *Robin Hood* took a dive, smokebox first, from the turntable, ending up in 2ft of water. Damage was slight and the engine was in service the next day. She was augmented in 1960 by a freelance Atlantic No 2005 *Black Prince* which had been designed and built by Curwen in 1952. The line was unusual in passing under a standard gauge railway line where the Great Western crossed Radipole Lake. Recalling the early history of Sunday trains in the Highlands, there was disquiet amongst some local people about the idea of the railway operating on the sabbath. But as a councillor observed, 'Is it anything new for railways to operate seven days a week?' A motion to limit the railway's operation was lost. The line is now closed and the track lifted; *Robin Hood*, seen here leaving the main station, may be found on the Oakhill Manor Miniature Railway. (*Thunder & Clayden Ltd*)

Above: Two $10\frac{1}{4}$in gauge railways in North Wales opened shortly after the second world war using locomotives built by Alfred Dove of Nottingham and under the same management. One, at Gwyrch Castle near Abergele, was operated by a freelance American 4-6-4 *President Eisenhower*, while the other, at Great Orme near Llandudno, was run by a similar engine *Commodore Vanderbilt*, seen here on 12 August 1953. The pipe on the chimney was to increase the draught when lighting up. *Commodore Vanderbilt* was built about 1948 and later went to the Skegness Miniature Railway which had opened on 10 August 1946, running from the Tower Esplanade along the Foreshore. (*H. C. Casserley*)

Left: The $10\frac{1}{4}$in gauge Hastings Miniature Railway was opened in 1947 on the beach at St Leonards, but in the following year it was transferred to its present site at Rock-a-Nore on the eastern end of Hastings beach. Much of the equipment came from the Marquis of Downshire's line at Easthampstead Park, including the Bassett-Lowke *Royal Scot* which had been sold to Captain Howey in 1946. This engine subsequently went to the Oakhill Miniature Railway on loan before moving to the USA. The line at Hastings, for many years associated with Ian Allan, has been extended to give a run of about 600yd. Here 0-6-0 *Firefly* is waiting to leave Rock-a-Nore station about 1970. Built in 1934 by Bullock as an 0-6-0PT for the Foxhill Miniature Railway, *Firefly* worked briefly on Bullock's miniature railway at Eversley before being returned to the FMR in 1937 on Bullock's death and was sold to Col Tyrrell to operate his line at Dymchurch. Rebuilt as a tender engine in 1946, *Firefly* worked on the original line at St Leonards in 1947, receiving a new boiler and wheels in 1951. (*G. M. Kichenside*)

$10\frac{1}{4}$in GAUGE IN PARKS AND LEISURE CENTRES

Above: The $10\frac{1}{4}$in gauge line around the park at Poole in Dorset was one of the railways started soon after the war by Southern Miniature Railways. Opened in 1948, the $\frac{1}{2}$ mile line was operated by a new freelance 4-4-2 No 1001 *Vanguard* built by SMR, a similar engine, No 1003 *Victory*, being built for the Southsea Miniature Railway which was also run by SMR. In 1965 the boiler of *Vanguard* was condemned which resulted in the engine being scrapped, an unusual occurrence with miniature locomotives. Since then the line has been operated by a diesel, although a petrol driven model of *Flying Scotsman*, which came from Tucktonia at Christchurch, began service at Poole in 1981. The two other SMR lines were at Southsea and Bognor Regis (formerly at Gosport). Steam no longer features at Southsea and the original Bognor line has closed. (*Mike Smith, Kelland Collection, BRC*)

Top right: Both LMS and LNER streamlined Pacifics are seldom the basis for a miniature locomotive. This example of LMS *Coronation* was built by Alfred Dove, a haulage contractor from Daybrook, Nottingham. The engine was completed in April 1946 and went to Ayr for a 16 week stint during which, according to the *Skegness News*, it pulled no fewer than 957,000 passengers! After this statistic, one is reluctant to put too much trust in the *Skegness News* report, but it stated that *Coronation* had reached 39.7mph on test, producing a drawbar pull of 25 tons! It appears that Dove used portable lines in seaside resorts and donated profits to charity. *Coronation* began running at Skegness in August 1946. In 1952 it was sold to N. H. Andrews for use on the Christchurch Miniature Railway which ran for a circuit of $\frac{1}{4}$ mile. Trains ran twice round on each trip. This photograph was taken at Christchurch on 20 July 1961. (*Mike Smith, Kelland Collection, BRC*)

Right: The seaside line at Cleethorpes is typical of many which have followed standard gauge practice and abandoned steam power, often after a change of ownership. Running for $\frac{3}{4}$ mile along the sea, the $10\frac{1}{4}$in gauge line was opened in 1948 by Botterills (who also ran the line at Hunstanton Pier) and operated by a pair of Carland Royal Scots and a Pacific by Dove of Nottingham. Unusually the line was converted to accumulator traction in 1954 but the line is now worked by a pair of Severn-Lamb Rio Grande 2-8-0 outline diesels. (*Author*)

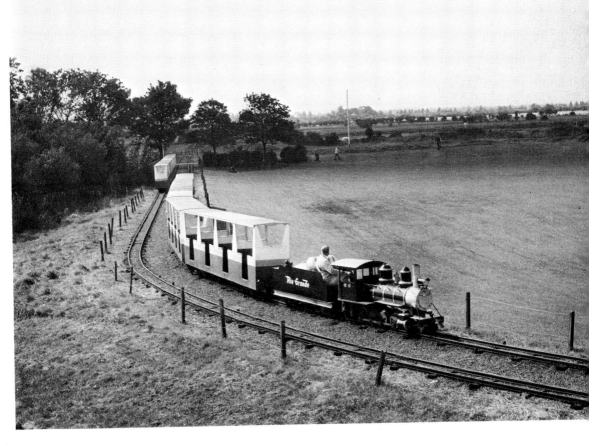

Above: One of the best-known miniature railways is the 10¼in gauge Stapleford Miniature Railway which connects the various attractions in the grounds of the sixteenth- /seventeenth-century mansion at Stapleford Park, Melton Mowbray. The first section of line, from Stable Hill station to what is now Central station, was opened on 18 May 1958 by the late Earl of Northesk. This section has since been abandoned. In 1960 the line was extended to the lake, serving the two Curwen-built paddle boats which give visitors a tour of the lake. A train-operated automatic level crossing was installed and Central station rebuilt at the same time. Motive power was provided by two Curwen Atlantics, *Blanche of Lancaster* and *John of Gaunt*, which had been built in 1948 and first run on the line at Bognor. The pair then went to Mablethorpe where they operated on a line round a field (not the present line on the sea front). A Royal Scot was completed in 1970, built by John Gretton and W. Whiteley, although this engine is now in Norfolk. The historic *Hampton Court*, a Great Western Saint 4-6-0 built by Twining in 1938, has recently been acquired from the Hastings Miniature Railway and will enter service after a rebuild. Seen here is another of the railway's English locomotives, LMS Jubilee 5565 *Victoria*, rebuilt from a Royal Scot by Coleby-Simkins. (*Tony Richardson*)

Right: John Gretton's admiration for the way American railroads tackled the innate operating and maintenance problems of steam locomotives has led to the construction of perhaps the finest miniature engine in the world. Built by Coleby-Simkins at Stapleford, the 2-8-4 Berkshire No 752 *The Lady Margaret* has conceded very little to the difficulties of reducing such a complex prototype to a scale of 2¼in to 1ft. In common with the full-size express freight engines which ran through the Berkshire Hills on the New York Central Railway, *The Lady Margaret* has a steam-driven mechanical stoker with air-operated firing jets for coal distribution in the firebox, two electric turbines for headlights and water gauge lights, two steam-driven duplex air compressors, a rocking grate and self-

discharging ashpan, air-operated firehole door, air-operated sanding equipment, all round mechanical lubrication by 26 pumps, heating coils on the lubricators, and compressed air brakes on the engine and tender with auxiliary steam brakes on the engine. Weighing $3\frac{1}{2}$ tons and almost 19ft long, No 752 has an all-welded BS class 1 boiler pressed to an exceptionally high 180lb/sq in. Even

The Lady Margaret, which was shown at The Model Engineer Exhibition in 1972, is likely to be eclipsed by the next locomotive from Stapleford's workshops: a Union Pacific 800 class 4-8-4 which is being built by John Wilks. It has already broken new ground by having a cast locomotive bed, complete with cylinders and air tanks, rather than fabricated frames.

Above: An illustration of the variation in size that can result from changing the scale of locomotive construction and taking a non-standard gauge prototype. Both engines are built for $10\frac{1}{4}$in gauge but the Denver & Rio Grande Western narrow gauge 2-8-2 No 489 was built to quarter scale whereas the GNR 4-4-2 No 4433 was built to one-sixth scale. The two engines are seen on the Audley End Miniature Railway, near Saffron Walden in Essex, which runs from a station opposite the drive to the early seventeenth-century mansion of Audley End. The line, which runs for about $\frac{3}{4}$ mile through woodland and returns to the station by a long return loop, was opened on 16 May 1964 by Stirling Moss. It was then a shorter run. The Rio Grande 2-8-2 was built by David Curwen and based on the engines that worked on the only *major* railroad in the USA to be laid to 3ft gauge. The GNR Atlantic was also built by Curwen, in 1963–5. A third steam engine, No 3548, a freelance North American type built by Curwen in 1948, used to operate on the historic line at Southend after it was regauged in 1952. (*Graham Ellis*)

Top right: Although the percentage of full-size A4s which have survived the cutter's torch is probably the highest of any class of locomotives (one-offs like CR No 123 obviously excepted), they are very rarely reproduced in miniature. An exception is this $10\frac{1}{4}$in A4, No 4498 *Sir Nigel Gresley*, built by W. Kirkland in 1967 and operating on a line of about $\frac{1}{3}$ mile at Thoresby Park near Ollerton. The whistle has been carefully made to reproduce the characteristic sound of an A4 whistle. (*Author*)

Right: Ian Allan, mostly through Ian Allan Miniature Railway Supplies Ltd, has, at various times, been involved in nine miniature railways. The privately-run Great Cockrow Railway at Chertsey is the only one worked primarily by steam and the only one still affiliated to its founder. Except for the Hastings Miniature Railway, which had one regular diesel locomotive amongst its otherwise steam fleet, the others were worked entirely by diesel mechanical or hydraulic locomotives. This is the line in Bognor Hotham Park opened in 1969, with Meteor 2, a 1-B-1 diesel-mechanical built by Shepperton Metal Products which later went to the Riverside Miniature Railway at Buckfastleigh where it was extensively rebuilt. The track at Hotham Park came from the short-lived $7\frac{1}{4}$/$10\frac{1}{4}$in line at Bassett's Manor, Hartfield, Sussex. The other Ian Allan lines were at Prestatyn, Whitby, Skegness, Sandown, Bognor Beaulieu Gardens (the only $7\frac{1}{4}$in line apart from the GCR), and two lines at Hastings — the Hastings Miniature Railway and a short-lived line in Alexandra Park. (*G. M. Kichenside*)

Above: It has been usual since the war for buses to replace a train service, but at Wells-next-the-Sea a $10\frac{1}{4}$in gauge miniature railway has replaced a bus. The Wells Harbour Railway links a large holiday camp at the beach with the town, saving a walk of almost a mile. Operating during Easter, at weekends until Spring Bank Holiday and then daily until the end of September, the line carries 45–50,000 passengers a year. Opened on 1 July 1976, the line is operated by 0-4-2 well tank *Edmund Hannay*, built by David King of Suffield, Norfolk, in 1972. The fixture on the running plate is a steam donkey pump for boiler feed. It is seen here on 10 September 1980. At the end of the 1980 season, it had run 48,000 miles. The owner of the line, Lt Commander R. W. Francis, has built a second line from Wells, to Walsingham, a distance of six miles which makes it the longest $10\frac{1}{4}$in line in the country. The track is laid on the bed of the GER Wells-Dereham line. (*Author*)

Right: The $10\frac{1}{4}$in gauge line which runs for $1\frac{1}{4}$ miles at the Age of Steam near Hayle in Cornwall was opened in May 1977 with diesel locomotives and much of the track from Sir Thomas Salt's line at Shillingstone in Dorset. The first steam engine, No 3 0-6-2T No 3 *Trevithick*, was built by Minimum Gauge Railways of Hinckley in 1975 and worked for a season at Stapleford while the Age of Steam was being built. The second engine No 4 *Isambard Kingdom Brunel* was built by David Curwen and delivered in June 1977. In 1978–9 No 4 was rebuilt with Walshaert's valve gear and a new boiler backhead. It is seen here with the cafe and exhibition building in the background on 31 August 1980. (*Author*)

Above: A 10¼in gauge one-third scale model built in 1974 by Coleby-Simkins Engineering of the Leek & Manifold 2-6-4T *E. R. Calthrop* which worked the 2ft 6in gauge railway from Waterhouses to Hulme End in Staffordshire. The miniature engine worked briefly on a line at Rudyard Lake in Staffordshire before moving to its present home in Suffolk. In company with a Royal Scot 4-6-0 built by Foden Tractors, it now operates on the line at Suffolk Wildlife Park at Kessingland near Lowestoft. The line forms a circuit with a loop through a wood and a terminus station in which waiting passengers can be entertained by a Wurlitzer cinema organ. (*Graham Ellis*)

Right: Without question the most bizarre miniature railway ever created was the 15in gauge line built at Battersea Park as part of the Festival of Britain in 1951. The Far Tottering & Oystercreek Railway of the *Punch* cartoonist Rowland Emmett became a reality with the extraordinary tunnel portal on the railway and the three diesel-electric locomotives built at Southport by S & B Miniature Railways Ltd. No 1 *Nellie* was built on the lines of the engine which featured in the cartoons, while No 2 *Neptune* represented an old paddle steamer, and No 3 *Wild Goose*, seen here, was based upon a hot air balloon. The locomotives hauled their four-coach trains over the ⅓ mile of track until 1953 when all the stock was returned to Southport. The line was relaid in Battersea Gardens, outside the Fun Fair, and re-opened with a pair of freelance streamlined Pacifics, powered by internal combustion engines, which had run at Porthcawl. (*H. C. Casserley*)

Top right: Mainstay of services at Oakhill Manor for several seasons has been Curwen Pacific *Robin Hood*, built in 1948 for the Weymouth Miniature Railway which was operated by Baydon Miniature Railway in association with David Curwen. *Robin Hood* ran at Audley End for a time before being put in store in the north. It was retrieved by Walter Harpur and remodelled to give it a more LNER appearance, although the wheels and motion were unaltered. An identical engine ran at Hillsea, then at Carr Mill in Lancashire; it is now in store in Lincolnshire. A Southern King Arthur 4-6-0 by H. Richards of North Wales arrived at Oakhill in 1980, and Great Western 47XX 2-8-0 by Keith Wilson is expected to arrive for the 1982 season. There are plans to extend the line at Oakhill, including the provision of return loops at both ends. (*Author*)

Overleaf: At Newby Hall near Ripon a particularly fine 10¼in gauge *Royal Scot*, built by J. Battinson in 1950, operates a ¾ mile line which was opened by Earl Mountbatten of Burma on 4 April 1971. Running through the gardens and orchards, the line offers many views of the adjacent River Ure and a glimpse of the hall itself up the long path that runs from the house to a landing stage. The opening of an extension in August 1979 was attended by Jackie Stewart who took the opportunity to drive the *Royal Scot*. Its regular driver is Eric Norfolk who not only maintains it in excellent condition but has replaced various non-functional parts which had been removed to make cleaning easier. A Severn-Lamb Western diesel, driven by a 1600cc cross flow Ford engine, supplements the *Royal Scot*. Stanley Battison also built three 9½in gauge Pacifics, which are now at Riber Castle, Matlock, and one, it is thought, in the USA. (*Author*)

Left: The 15in gauge Blenheim Palace Miniature Railway was opened by Pleasurerail on Spring Bank Holiday in 1975. The Pacific, appropriately named *Sir Winston Churchill*, was built as a 4-6-0 in 1950 by Trevor Guest of Stourbridge, based on a Stanier Class 5 (Trevor Guest also completed a $10\frac{1}{4}$in Class 5 in 1950, which ran at Rhyl and Lowestoft). The 15in Class 5 ran at Dudley Zoo as *Prince Charles* until 1957 when it was taken out of service and stored until being placed on loan to the Fairbourne Railway in 1960. In 1962 *Prince Charles* returned to Stourbridge for rebuilding by Guest, emerging as a 4-6-2 with more than a passing resemblance to the Fairbourne's Pacific *Ernest W. Twining* which had been built by Guest to Twining's design in 1949. Several years in store followed rebuilding until *Prince Charles* was purchased by W. H. McAlpine who, as Chairman of Pleasurerail, returned it to service at Blenheim as *Sir Winston Churchill*. (*P. H. Groom*)

Above: Situated on the Yorkshire bank of the River Tees three miles downstream from Barnard Castle, the 15in gauge Whorlton Lido Miniature Railway was opened at Easter 1971 with Bassett-Lowke Class 20 *King George V*, formerly *Prince of Wales* when at Llewelyn's Miniature Railway, Southport. The railway is in the shape of a ham bone, giving a $\frac{1}{2}$-mile run in a delightful setting, and incorporates a 33yd tunnel which serves as a carriage shed. Apart from the beauty of the natural surroundings, the line has been particularly well landscaped and standard gauge signals are used. *King George V*, seen here, is augmented by a diesel mechanical Bo-Bo named *Wendy* which was assembled by Messrs Coleby-Simkins from parts supplied by the railway's owner, Raymond R. Dunn. Mr Dunn's father had operated lines at Saltburn, Seaton Carew and Crimdon Dean. Between 1976 and May 1979, the line was host to the magnificent three-cylinder *Flying Scotsman* built by W. P. Stewart which may be seen in a photograph on page 29. (*G. T. Heavyside*)

NEW 15in GAUGE LINES

Top left: The Bird Paradise at Hayle in Cornwall has a 15in gauge circuit of about $\frac{1}{4}$ mile in the grounds. Opened in 1976, the line is worked by an 0-4-0 built in 1968 in Amsterdam. Before coming to Hayle in 1978, *Chough* was stored at New Romney. (*Author*)

Left: The 15in gauge Lappa Valley Railway from Benny Halt to East Wheal Rose was opened in June 1974 along the trackbed of the GWR Newquay-Chacewater branch which closed in 1963. At the end of the one mile journey are the remains of the silver and lead mine which once employed over 1,200 people. The mine suffered a tragedy in 1846 when 39 people were drowned following torrential rain which defeated the pumps. The mine later had the distinction of owning one of the largest pumping engines in the country: the cylinder was so large that 13 people sat down to dinner inside it to commemorate its installation. The first engine on the 15in line was Severn-Lamb 0-6-2T *Zebedee*, sister to *Dougal* on the Longleat Railway and fitted with Baker valve gear. The second engine seen here was *Muffin*, an 0-6-0 designed by David Curwen and built by Berwyn Engineering in 1967, formerly on the Longleat Railway. (*Author*)

Above: Little Giant No 18 *George the Fifth* at Longleat before renaming by Mrs Elenora Steel, *née* Greenly, on 15 October 1978. *George the Fifth* was built in 1911 for the line at Southport but was sold to Rhyl after the Improved Little Giant No 21 *Prince Edward of Wales* arrived at Southport in 1912. After nine years at Rhyl, No 18 went to Skegness and Southend before its longest service on one railway, at Belle Vue, Manchester. It was under a pile of scrap metal there that Robin Butterell found it in 1964, nine years after being taken out of service. Purchased and restored by Robin Butterell and John Milner, *George the Fifth* is now at Steamtown, Carnforth. (*Author*)

Above: The 15in gauge railway at Steamtown, Carnforth, began as a portable line of about 200yd in 1975/6, using a much rebuilt Bassett-Lowke Class 20 Improved Little Giant No 22 *Princess Elizabeth* (originally *Prince of Wales*). In the autumn of 1977 the line was moved to the west side of the site and extended by 150yd. The rolling stock went in August 1978 to an exhibition in Newcastle where it was pulled by Barnes Atlantic *Joan* which then returned to work at Steamtown for three months. With the help of a Job Creation Project, the line has been extended to 1200yd, incorporating a four-road engine shed with traverser, three stations and a 'tunnel' through the standard gauge engine shed. *Princess Elizabeth*, seen here with the first train of the day, shares duties with Class 10 Little Giant No 18 *George the Fifth*, seen on page 93 before moving to Carnforth. (*D. Rodgers*)

Top right: The 6in gauge of this line at the Southern Railway Homes for Children at Woking in Surrey is thought to be unique. The gauge is almost on the lower limit capable of supporting a human being without raising the track off the ground to lower the centre of gravity of the passengers; Sir Berkeley Sheffield's line at his home in Lincolnshire, Normandy Park, was only $4\frac{3}{4}$in gauge, and passengers sat on, rather than astride, the wagons that passed for coaches on the line. Such a narrow gauge could hardly be considered satisfactory without elevation of the track as the ride would inevitably be uncomfortable and the train liable to tip over if a passenger leaned to one side. The discomfort of the driver is evident from the angle of his legs although his position would have been eased by having foot rests on the engine. The locomotive is a freelance 4-6-2 interpretation of a Southern Railway Lord Nelson class 4-6-0. (*G. M. Kichenside*)

Right: One of the most elaborately conceived miniature railways ever built was the $12\frac{1}{4}$in gauge Réseau Guerlédan, sited on the trackbed of the former metre gauge Reseau Breton between Mur-de-Bretagne and Caurel in the Côtes du Nord. Despite its location, the railway was an entirely British affair, built by John de Vries Ellerton and using equipment supplied by British companies. Construction of the 5km line began in October 1977, enabling passenger services to commence in May 1978 with a replica of a Rio Grande Southern 'Galloping Goose', built by David Curwen. The first steam engine arrived in the following month, a half-size model of a Darjeeling-Himalaya Railway 0-4-0 saddle tank, *France* built by Milner Engineering, which handled the rest of the season's traffic unaided. For 1979, *France* was supplemented by a Curwen-built 2-6-2T *Jubilee*, based on the Lynton & Barnstaple Railway Manning Wardle prototypes, although employing Walschaerts valve gear rather than the Joy system of the original. If the reality was splendid enough, the prospects were extraordinary: the locomotives planned included a Leek & Manifold 2-6-4T, an 0-6-4T based on the North Wales Narrow Gauge Railway's *Beddgelert*, a Shay and a Denver & Rio Grande Western 2-8-2. Tragically circumstances conspired against a steady development of the railway's potential and it was closed at the end of the 1979 season. Today the line is no more and the equipment is currently stored in packing cases. It can only be hoped that a future will be secured for the exceptional products of a brilliant conception. This photograph of the 'Darj' waiting to leave Mur-de-Bretagne shows the large six road locomotive carriage and wagon shed and one of the ten coaches based on the Festiniog Railway end-balcony vehicles (*Everil Hollingsworth*)

A MISCELLANY

The 12$\frac{1}{4}$in gauge of the Littlehampton Miniature Railway is thought to be unique and is the result of a decision by Mr Cookson, when rebuilding two 10$\frac{1}{4}$in Bullock 4-6-4 tank engines, that an extra 2in would give much better stability. These two engines, with which the 900yd, S-shaped line opened in 1948, have been supplemented by two Atlantics, one built by Bullock and the other by Flooks in 1938. (*H. C. Casserley collection*)

ACKNOWLEDGEMENTS

One of the final tasks of the non-fiction author is the list of acknowledgements. It is a welcome opportunity of thanking the many people who have contributed to the book by providing photographs, or reminiscences, or generous hospitality. To the following I extend my gratitude: Messrs M. E. Arnold, H. Armitage, J. Ballantine Dykes, A. D. Barlow, G. Barlow, K. Beeley, R. B. Beggs, D. G. Bell, W. G. Belsher, C. J. Bishop, P. J. Bottrill, J. I. C. Boyd, D. Bromwich, Mrs U. Budd, Mr R. Butterell, Mrs L. J. Byers, Mr W. A. Camwell, Miss F. J. Cargill, Messrs H. C. Casserley, R. E. J. Compton, M. E. Corbett, W. J. Croft, K. Q. Crook, Miss J. Curtis, Messrs A. D. Dodds, R. R. Dunn, T. J. Edgington, G. Ellis, W. Evans, D. Ferreira, N. Fields, Lt Commander R. W. Francis, Mr L. L. Gore, The Hon J. Gretton, Messrs T. Graham, J. Gray, P. H Groom, Miss K. M. Guest, Messrs J. F. Hall Craggs, M. Hanson, W. Harper, D. E. Harrison D. Hayler, J. Haylock, G. T. Heavyside J. Hollick, Mr & Mrs J. B. Hollingsworth, M. J. Howson, Mrs B. Hudson, Messrs E. Hughes W. Hunt, Sir Leslie Joseph, Messrs M. B. Kerr G. M. Kichenside, W. Kirkland, A. Leach, the Earl of Leicester, Mrs G. Leitch, Messrs D. Lloyd F. W. Manders, R. Marsh, B. L. Merrifield, M. R Oliver, T. A. Owen, J. F. C. Powys, S. C Pritchard, R. G. Roberts, D. C. Rodgers, D. T Roy, A. C. Schwab, W. R. Serjeant, M. Smith S. Smith, J. B. Snell, J. Southern, Mr & Mrs E. A Steel, Messrs J. Tidmarsh, J. Turner, S. Weighell R. White, C. M. Whitehouse, J. K. Williams, and K. Wilson.